Hieronymus Bosch: his life and works

Archival records mention Hieronymus Bosch for the first time around 1480. By this time Bosch had already married a wealthy patrician's daughter and had completed his formal studies of painting. He was around twenty-five years old and shortly to enter The Brotherhood of Our Lady. Bosch came from a town in Holland called Hertogenbosch, the name of which he adopted as a nom de plume. His surname can be traced back to the late 14th century in Hertogenbosch and suggests that his predecessors originated from Aix-la-Chapelle. Bosch was the child of a supposedly very well-known family of artists who, however, never managed to step out of the shadows of their local area. Although his mother was a dressmaker, Bosch numbered among the most respected members of his home community, thanks to his marriage and his membership of the Brotherhood of Our Lady which was close to the Church. In 1496 Bosch became acquainted with the rich and influential Jew Jacob de Almaengien who underwent baptism in the presence of Philip the Fair and simultaneously became a member of the Brotherhood. Although sources are reticent on the subject of the relationship between Bosch and Jacob/Philip, this meeting must have represented an important incision in the life of a painter almost unknown until then. Philip's sister, Margaret of Austria, was regent of the Netherlands and had a residence in Mechlin. It seems certain that Bosch now maintained close contact with the Court and thus not only received numerous commissions but also made a career in society. Although the term "Court Painter" cannot be applied to the circumstances of those times and is not employed in the records, it can be assumed that Bosch enjoyed a similar status. In these noble gentlemen he found patrons who allowed him to translate all his creative energies into action. As for the influence of Jacob de Almaengien, we must rely for the most part on conjecture. He was certainly an influential businessman, widely travelled and well acquainted, thanks to his former faith and his origins, with the newest scientific and intellectual developments. To what extent Jacob was a member of free sects and brotherhoods cannot be proved conclusively. But sources assume that Bosch, over and above his deep faith, on the one hand, and sharp analytical intellect on the other, did not quite shut himself off from the ideas of the Grand Master. The written records from those times inform us that Bosch was introduced by him to the realms of freethinking which then found expression in such a fantastic way in his paintings. Since the 16th century rash rumours have been spreading about whether and to what extent Bosch himself was a member of various secret societies and sects. Without doubt, the extraordinary and even today largely unfathomable creative energy of the Master, as well as the completely new images in his paintings, explain attempts to associate him with heretical peripheral groupings, although no conclusive proof has been provided. In his patrons, however, he must have found understanding and intellectually progressive admirers, for they represent his most important customers alongside the Brotherhood. As early as 1510 his works appeared in famous collections in Europe, for example Madrid, Venice and Brussels. On 9 August 1516 the funeral mass of Hieronymus Bosch was read. Apart from few rare dates and facts very little is known to us of the life of Bosch, and for this very reason an improbably large number of rumours, speculations and stories have spread about his person and even more so about his unique oeuvre. Although Bosch was a descendant of an old family of artists who quickly found respect, riches and success, not a single source has been passed down to us in which he comments on his life, his customers, his friends and, most importantly, his work. For this reason too, an exact dating of his paintings is scarcely possible. In contrast to Leonardo da Vinci, who was not only a contemporary of Bosch but also resembles him in terms of richness of ideas and creative energy, and who left behind hundreds of documents from his period of productivity, we find that in order to interpret the paintings of Bosch we must rely on no other information than the pictures themselves.

Just as unfathomable as the life of Bosch will remain of his extensive artistic work and his inner motivation. His cycles of paintings have such far-reaching symbolic and allegorical dimensions, are so encyclopedic and visionary that generations of busy researchers were not able to offer us a comprehensive explanation of Bosch's paintings. In the first instance Bosch tackles the portrayal of the lives of the saints, he then devotes himself to a description of the Passion of Christ, and finally he moves over towards new ways of interpreting the Last Day. Until this point a strict canon of prescribed forms, drawn up gradually in the course of the centuries and hardly ever modified, had determined the treatment of such themes closely connected with Church teaching. Artists were answerable to a strict hierarchical system and to the dogmatic teachings of the Church. Changes took effect only very hesitantly, such that artists found little opportunity to change their interpretation of traditional themes to any significant extent. A "Madonna", a "St. John", a "Last Day" were all subject to the same strict laws, and only minimal variations in the treatment of perspective, space and above all landscapes were tolerated by the strict eye of the Church and State.

Bosch, as a child of the impending Modern Era, breaks away from the familiar images in pictures and revolutionizes painting in his own impetuous and imaginative way. Before long, slander and defamation and other infamous attacks – alongside clueless admiration – constantly accompany his path and work. Suddenly, for example, he presents the "Last Day" no longer in accustomed form; instead he replaces the court scene with a "Hay Wain" which is pulled by all kinds of foolish men and demons. The "Last Day" thus becomes an allegorical portrayal of the vices and sins of mankind. Bosch takes biblical themes and alters their message little by little inasmuch as he places man at the centre of his work. In this point he differs, of course, from the Middle Ages which had seen man as a completely subordinate being. If man is now present in a realistic form in Bosch's work, in the interest of his interpretation, then this is in keeping with the Renaissance. Yet it should be noted that, in the visual arts of the Italian Renaissance, that same man is to be seen as the embodiment of the splendour of creation. He is the highpoint of creation, a being which can shape creatively and which has taken his fate into his own hands, independent of the Church and State. Bosch centres his attention on man too, but in the form of his vices, his boundless stupidity and his sins. To make this contrast clear, Bosch separates his portrayal of the world from that of man, a process which at first seemed impossible in the Italian Renaissance. For Bosch the landscape is either a world functioning according to cosmic laws but not to any set of values, and which thus hardly has anything in common with man, or it is a fantastic and allegorical portrayal of an exaggerated elaborateness with the task of elucidating the vices of mankind and all their consequences.

The boldness of the fantastically grotesque architecture portrayed underlines the significance of the landscape in his pictures. These visions have nothing to do with the natural world. Flora and fauna are used in the same way by Bosch in his pictures. They do not belong to the world formed by "Creation" but are subject to the same mad laws as nature, architecture and mankind. Evolution has been abolished. Everything is possible. Architecture mingles with vegetation, and nature is architecturalized, or at least is helped towards an artificial state which recalls the alteration of physical and chemical states of aggregation in Bosch's pictures. Bosch alters in this way not just nature but also the world created according to physical laws known to him. Neither gravity nor age, neither birth nor death operate in keeping with their inherent regular patterns. These absurd and frightening images find expression thanks to an incredible imagination which is hardly explicable, unless with the assistance of modern psychology, medicine and the interpretation of dreams, although even these sciences can offer only partial explanations.

It is certain that Bosch, with his imaginative world, did not only address the fears of his times but also the longings and desires forbidden by taboos and the Church. Using famous proverbs and sayings as his point of departure, Bosch begins to illustrate literary and popular customs and conventions, but without forgetting to interpret these too as a symbol of human foolishness and evil. All the various yearnings and urges inherent in man are portrayed, indeed they become the insignia of Bosch's pictures. For him human beings are not individuals but parts of an indefinable mass, with the result that he cannot permit them to come into their own as personalities which can be differentiated; instead he presents typical physiognomies, a characteristic which on the one hand is reminiscent of the Middle Ages, and on the other runs counter to the advances of the Italian Renaissance. Whether in his allegories of this world such as "The Ship of Fools" and "The Cure of Folly" or in his sacral themes such as the "Deadly Sins" or the lives of the saints – Bosch is hardly interested in the portrait-like illustration of people known to him. All those bodies and faces become detached from their owners and represent mere incarnations of the basic qualities typically present in man; Bosch divides these into vices and sins. By illustrating human characters which can neither suffer nor enjoy themselves, Bosch unbuilds the human personality in the same way as he had treated nature. So we are obliged to see here not so much human beings somewhere between paradise, earth, and hell, as spiritual conditions. Bosch paints souls on their inevitable path from good to evil. As discussed in the "Hay Wain", the soul finds itself on a journey from paradise to hell, or to purgatory, and only during the short stay on earth is there the chance to decide in favour of God and paradise. Mankind, led by the devil, does not succeed in this task, however, and as though on a "Ship of Fools" man in this world is on course for destruction. Alongside "Creation" we can thus discern in Bosch's work a pessimistic existential fear similar to that fear experienced by modern man in the face of atomic destruction, genetic engineering and new diseases. Above all, Bosch's pictures contain a certain irony and splendid naivety which will always stimulate our imagination in a positive fashion.

The illustrations

Please note: the commentaries on pages 4 to 14 are presented in a sequence which allows the reader to follow the author's development of ideas related to the illustrations.

33 Christ carrying the Cross

Oil on panel, 57.2 x 32 cm. Vienna, Kunsthistorisches Museum

"Christ carrying the Cross" is one of Bosch's later works and can be seen as part of that area of pictorial art which has as its thematic common denominator the portrayal of traditional biblical events. "Christ carrying the Cross", "The Mocking of Christ" and "Christ presented to the People" describe the Passion of Christ, but also, at the same time, the hate, envy, and violence displayed by man not only towards Christ but his fellow citizens too. Whereas until around 1450 biblical themes more or less had the purpose of conveying the message of Holy Scripture like a story to those unable to read for themselves, these portrayals develop to become a vehicle for the presentation of human vices and inadequacies. The action thus serves in the first instance as a mask for a concealed indictment. Again and again, not only in Bosch's work, we find this "secularization" of the modes of presentation prescribed by the Church; this process was of course exposed to attacks from the Church's institutions. The Inquisition kept a strict guard to ensure that sacred themes did not become a vehicle for questioning teachings and dogma; indeed, not just Christian teaching but man in general was defended in this way. Numerous painters had to pay from time to time for their concealed openness in the form of defamation, torture, or death.

An overlapping technique in keeping with the accustomed medieval tradition characterizes Bosch's picture; the actual centre of the picture, however, is almost lost in favour of parallel incidents in the foreground. The wretchedness of the story is emphasized by the nondescript landscape in the background. A crowd of people, moving spiritedly, threatens to crush Christ who is staggering. As in many of Bosch's pictures, the artist concentrates here too on an immoderate characterization of those ignoble qualities which he presents again and again: stupidity, hatred, violence, flippancy, and stubbornness. Moreover, the drama of "Christ carrying the Cross" is further underlined by the emblem of the toad on the shield of the warrior in front of Jesus. The fat toad marks the tormentors as a people of the devil with whom Christ wishes to have nothing to do. He bows his humiliated head and closes his eyes in face of the diabolical evil of man. In contrast, his companions in adversity stand at the bottom of the picture, fainthearted and pitiable as they await their crucifixion.

15 Christ carrying the Cross

Oil on panel, 76.5 x 83.5 cm. Ghent, Musée des Beaux-Arts

When compared to the Viennese portrayal of "Christ carrying the Cross" (33), this picture seems like an enlargement of the scene painted in the top half of that work: the face of Christ appears surrounded by a number of grotesque heads, but it remains unclear how God the Son is actually carrying the heavy cross – an indication perhaps of how Bosch is not as interested in the actual historical event as in the symbolism, the coded message of the incident. If we speak in terms of an enlargement, then surely less in the sense of an optical than of a human variation on the Viennese picture. Here too the artist aims to use a biblical theme as a vehicle for giving an account of human vices in general, an intention which can be counted among the central characteristics of Bosch's pictures.

The experienced artist and gifted observer dares the unprecedented, but superb, move of presenting opposite the sanctity of Christ a colourful palette of human characters and physiognomies. This description and this contrast correspond to the deeper meaning of the dramatic action: at the centre we see, untouched and spiritualized, a dreaming Redeemer who has closed his eyes in order not to have to observe the human evil which surrounds him. Closer inspection will show that his eyes, his promise, can in fact be identified in the painting, i.e. in the veil of St Veronica; she too closes her eyes and turns her delicate head away from the demonic murderers in the black, hellish background. Only at this point does the meaning of the parable become apparent: whereas the infernal grimacing faces surrender themselves completely to their own ugliness, hatred, and evil, and thus degrade the observer who feels like a voyeur, Christ, in the left half of the picture, turns gently to the spectator, as if to warn him to keep his distance from the tormentors, but also from sin in general. Finally, the beginnings of a genre can be seen in this picture which stands in direct contrast to the aesthetic ideal image of Renaissance Man (Raffael, Michelangelo): the caricature, which was to find one of its first highlights in the art of Mannerism.

16 Christ carrying the Cross

Oil on panel, 150 x 94 cm. Madrid, Royal Palace

Unlike both other portrayals of "Christ carrying the Cross" (55, 33), this picture is unusually large; once again a scene from Christ's bitter path to the cross is, as it were, picked out and portrayed as large as life. The landscape, bathed in a cold green, shows, as in the painting "Christ presented to the People" (34), a rich and powerful Netherlandish town before the far-reaching and melancholy lowlands of Holland known to us from paintings of the 16th and 17th centuries. The mighty tower is a cross between a fortress, such as can be found all over France (Donjon), and a cathedral dome, and is thus reminiscent of the Tower of Babel and the decline of that town. Bosch describes at the centre of his impressive picture not the fall of a town, but the fall, the curse of man who has succumbed to the devil. In the foolish procession citizens of all social classes have gathered to lead Christ to his crucifixion. New and original in this case is, of course, the manner in which the artist narrates this incredible incident against the background of the town: a deeply human portrayal, as if it were a pictorial presentation of the biblical proverb "Every man has his own cross to bear". On the other hand, the suggestion has also been made that the painting contains a symbolical allusion to man's path through life, a way of the cross which can lead from original sin in paradise to God. This ambivalence, pointing on the one hand to the suffering of man seduced by the devil, but on the other hand also to the brutal violence of which we are capable, is new among Bosch's skilful modes of presentation. Faced with this picture, as with life, we can decide: do we wish to identify with the vain, avaricious and demon-like murderers, or with Christ who carries the large and heavy cross apparently without any effort although he seems to fall. Jesus is pained not by the whip of the figure which resembles St Peter, nor by the cross, but by his worries about the path taken by man who, in the final analysis, lets him stumble. He is the only person in this group to give us a questioning and at the same time warning look – as though he wanted to know our decision!

34 Christ presented to the People

Oil on panel, 75 x 61 cm. Frankfurt, Städelsches Kunstinstitut

Together with the various portrayals of "Christ carrying the Cross", the painting "Christ presented to the People" treats too of the theme of the Passion of Christ. In contrast to the other paintings, however, the action here is embedded in a spacious and elegant town characterized by artistic architecture.

While Christ's murderers – beneath a stone platform – and the High Priests who stand like City Fathers on the platform before the Court of Justice look like the faces portrayed in the versions of "Christ carrying the Cross", a curious contrast unfolds between these grotesque figures and the supposedly attractive town and surrounding landscape. So we are obliged not just to note the contrast between the citizens of this world, marked by vanity, greed, and hatred, and the Redeemer from above, but also the contrast between this terrible story and the urbane town in the background. "Urbane" – polite, elegant – should be interpreted symbolically here, as a quality of the town. We know this type of presentation already from scenes, flooded with light, of the Italian Renaissance. Although this rich town of stone appears to lead a peaceable existence, Bosch undermines this impression with the symbolically red town flag. The crescent (Turkey) is a mark of the unchristianness of the town and thus of its inhabitants – an allegory which has become a shameful reality in the foreground. Christ was presented to his tormentors not only in Jerusalem, but also in Bosch's times, and even today, for here too Christ is a symbol for those men who, day after day, must experience suffering and hatred at the hands of their fellow men. In the action portrayed, the vote of the crowd for the death of Christ, that fanaticism and hatred find expression about which some people complain again and again in our own times, and for this reason this little picture seems to give a timely and topical warning. The people in the painting represent all the social ranks in the town, including the clergy, and it would seem that Bosch is making an indictment here, that he is first to paint what only few people had dared to utter; he anticipates the Reformation, not as the member of a sect (of which he was accused constantly) but as a human being.

35 Christ before Pilate

Oil on panel, 84.5 x 108 cm. New Jersey, USA, Princeton Art Museum

In this painting there is no accompanying landscape which comments on the central image. Bosch concentrates here on the description of those protagonists around Christ and the High Priest Pilate. Although he once again selects a story from the New Testament and portrays this expressively, Bosch is not so much interested in historical fact; instead he uses the incident as an excuse to explore more closely the characteristics and physiognomy of the actors. Once again there is a striking contrast between the relaxed figure of Christ and Pilate who wants to wash his hands in innocence and the grimacing sneers of those contemporaries who will soon torment him. Jesus sits in formal robes, his eyes closed, his hands crossed, before Pilate who raises his hand in a warning gesture as if he wishes to distance himself from the judgement and consequent horrors. In keeping with the formal dress of Christ is the rudiment of a late Gothic window, fragments of which can be identified in both top corners – a reference to Pilate's Palace of Justice, or to a church in which the action takes place, not just at the time of Christ but also in the present of the artist. We can expand this to say that the moral indictment made here by Bosch is directed at his times, at his fellow citizens, and at the rulers: this fact finds confirmation in many other paintings by Bosch. The silver key before Pilate, an exclusive privilege of the very rich, is in keeping too with the distinguished setting.

Christ anticipates in unbroken silence those things

HIERONYMUS BOSCH

Michael M. Stanić

TIGER BOOKS INTERNATIONAL
LONDON

© 1988 by I.P. Verlagsgesellschaft
International Publishing GmbH., München
Published in 1988 for
Tiger Books International Limited, London
ISBN 1-870461-59-2
Printed and bound by Brepols N.V.-Turnhout, Belgium
Translation: Donal McLaughlin

which irrevocably await him and he takes no cognizance of the citizens who surround him. Bosch devotes himself to these people in a quite unusual way. Nowhere in the painting of past centuries do such distorted and grotesque human faces congregate, although the composition of the picture is certainly of traditional Italian origin, as is the portrayal of the elegant setting. Fragments of human caricatures, escapees from a diabolical lunatic asylum, are depicted here, and they are not even in a position to torment and crucify Christ.

17 The Mocking of Christ

Oil on panel, 72.5 x 58.5 cm. London, National Gallery.

This painting, too, does without an accompanying landscape and "eloquent architecture". Bosch devotes himself solely to the torments of the crowning of thorns. Since late medieval tradition is his point of departure, the composition is strictly symmetrical and reflects an inner order which we know from Italian paintings of the 15th and 16th centuries. This order, however, is no indication of the harmony, beauty and truth of a situation – as was usual in Italy until that date – but solely the interpretation of another truth: of the terrible fact that behind the elegant and very proper external appearance of the murderers lies concealed something deeply saddening.

Once more Bosch takes an historical biblical event as an excuse to examine the relationship between man and his fellow human beings. The spectator, with whom Christ seems to speak, perceives – assuming his soul is open to the Holy Message – the indictment made in the first instance by Jesus himself and then by the artist too. Compared to the grimaces and sneers in Illustration 15, the protagonists here seem to be more composed, indeed the torturers depicted at the top of the picture appear to display sympathy. Yet behind these masks too – unlike in other variations – lie concealed in even more drastic form brutality, violence, presumption, and hostility. Bosch varies, in a manner both exceedingly dramatic and simultaneously most artistic, his condemnation and personal experience of life. Behind the mask and facade of the apparent nobility too lurks the unprecedented violence which Christ experiences here as the representative of all mistreated individuals. His bright gown, which is being ripped from his body, stands out noticeably against the dark, broken colours of the myrmidons who prepare to humiliate Christ with instruments of torture. The mildness in his face, however, seems to advise those individuals mistreated then and today as to how to live according to his teaching. Alongside the clear condemnation of the artist we find here a way out of the Vale of Tears which is our world: Christ himself.

18 The Marriage at Cana

Oil on panel, 93 x 72 cm. Rotterdam, Museum Boymans-van Beuningen

At first sight it appears that nothing extraordinary is depicted in this painting. A distinguished wedding party has congregated in an elegant palace to celebrate the marriage of a couple. Upon closer inspection, however, we become aware of a few peculiarities which point to a deeper significance and symbolism. This technique of leading the spectator beyond his first impressions towards deeper layers of meaning and truth is characteristic not just of Bosch but of the painting of recent centuries. The pictures of Bosch in particular must be decoded nowadays, for their content is not immediately accessible.

Despite the distinguished decoration of the palace no real space is actually depicted. As in a stage setting, the fragile decoration consists of various components. The fragile interior decoration consists of various individual elements too, and is thus reminiscent of comparable stage settings. Brocade curtains at a slant and wallpapered partitions lead the spectator's uneasy gaze towards a window with railings and a strange platform (left) at the top of the painting. The Gothic apse with the completely illogical dome and pillars puzzles the eye too. The impression is gained that this architectural fragment was taken from earlier miniature paintings. At the same time we are unsure about the location of this chapel – is this meant to be a church or a palace? – for curious things are happening both in it and at the high table. We can assume that Bosch was more than capable of depicting "real" architecture but that he wished to confuse the senses of the spectator, for there is something crazy about this frivolous story into which the guests themselves lead us.

The arrangement of the guests, just like the architecture, yields the deceptive impression of order in the first instance; the composition seems to take up a tradition which goes back to Giotto and which since the 13th century has been part of the standard canon of modes of presentation for the Marriage at Cana. Mary, the bride (at the centre of the picture), Christ (to the right, giving a blessing), and a monk to his left represent the real marriage at Cana and mingle as representatives of Good among the other people. These may give the impression of being distinguished company, but they are all heretics. They surrender themselves to gluttony, wine, magic (conjurer in the chapel) and other base lusts, and desecrate not only the setting but also the sacrament of marriage. Intentionally, Bosch here presents the good and the bad virtues alongside each other, they find expression in the faces and gestures of the citizens; in the end he leaves it to the spectator to decide in favour of Good or Evil. The sacred actions of Christ, his miracle, and the Eucharist, portrayed here together for the first time, are perverted by the self-indulgence and the primitive sensuality of the wedding guests. Objects on the altar and high table which are actually holy and blessed symbols of the Eucharist are re-cast to become symbols of heresy and vice – in a manner, of course, which permits of both interpretations, depending on which section of the party attracts the spectator. Bosch allows us the freedom to act as we wish – in the event that we have recognized the ambiguity of the allegory – although his concealed indictment must now seem unmistakable.

36/37 Paradise and Hell

Oil on panel, 34.5 x 21 cm, and 33.4 x 19.6 cm, New York, Wildenstein Gallery

Both wings were once part of a triptych in which the central compartment portrayed the "Last Day" but is no longer extant. The themes of the wings – paradise (left wing) and hell (right) – can only be understood in terms of the action, or rather the inescapable consequences of the court, and only in this connection do they take on their brisant quality and powerful expression (cf "The Last Day", 20, 21, 38–43). The tiny paintings are approximately the size of an A4 page and represent the early period of the Master, as is underlined by the simple depiction of the figures and by landscapes which are not yet worked out to the last detail; this style corresponds to medieval techniques which emphasized not so much the exact and thorough depiction of the protagonists, but more their symbolic qualities. The painting expresses a great truth with faces suggestive of a high spiritual refinement and this determines the character of the applied technique. Fragments of this technique always remained in Bosch's work and even later in his development he consciously employed them as an artistic option. Worthy of note in this respect is the fact that objects and figures in Bosch's paintings rarely cast shadows. In this way the Master removes them from this earthly world and in part gives them a new atomicity; this stylistic technique was later perfected by Breughel.

"Paradise" and "Hell", as already suggested, can only be seen in the context of the "Last Day", and triptychs of this kind should be viewed from left to right. From the promise of paradise the eye wanders across to the Last Day on which, for the believing Christian, the unyielding decision falls to which his whole life on earth is geared. The fear of hell with its threat of terrible tortures was supposed at that time to give man a drastic impression of how his life would end if he strayed from the path of virtue.

But not only the content of the painting stresses the contrast between Heaven and Hell. Bosch employs contrasting colours as a further stylistic technique which marks the differences between the two wings even from a distance. The background landscape, pleasing to the eye with a sailing craft passing by leisurely, is presented in delicate blues and greens in a manner known to us from Italian landscapes of the 15th century. The happy mood of the painting has its centre in terms of colour in the cool and refreshing white and blue of the tent in the foreground, in front of which naked human beings take pleasure in being alive. The harmonious triad of colour is made complete by the delicate pink of the canopy above the boat and the angel's cloak. Wherever you look, these believers enjoy the fruits of their faithful earthly existence, they frisk about in the mild climate of the "Paysage" which permits them to be unclothed. This is an ancient, ideal picture of paradise, of a spacious Garden of Eden, just as can be found in the earliest works of European painting. The artists' imagination works in part on literary sources and descriptions of paradise, and of course of hell (e.g. Dante's "Divina Comedia"). The colours of hell are brown and black, and these cause the spectator verily to shudder, especially if he first focuses on the luminous pink and grey-blue of the bedcover and surrounds. This internal contrast leads the eye to the central event: in a bed of state, the privilege of the rich on earth, an apparently young woman tries to defend herself against lizards, toads, and snakes which close in on her. On the baldachin, dragon-like figures attack another human being who, defenceless and naked, is exposed to his tormentors. In the background we see a town wall with a flag which once again shows a toad. As such this town is marked as a homestead of the devil, in contrast to the ideal image of the town as paradise on the other wing. For some time already notions of paradise – "New Jerusalem" – and hell had been linked with the model of cities. This is seen in the recurring symbols of tent, tower, gates, fences etc. Of course, images of a paradisiacal town and garden are often superimposed, though both are then of the same origin.

38–41 The Last Day

Oil on panel, central compartment 163.7 x 127 cm; wings 167.7 x 160 (80) cm. Vienna, Galerie der Akademie der Bildenden Künste

"The Last Day", like all great triptychs, consists of three parts: of the central compartment with its depiction of the "Last Day" and of both wings which, according to need, could be opened or closed to present or conceal the central portion. Paradise is depicted on the left wing, hell on the right.

"The Last Day" is part of a series of large triptychs created by Bosch. Also included in this series are another version of "The Last Day" (20, 21, 42, 43), "The Hay Wain" (27, 28, 29, 54–56), "The Temptation of St Anthony" (24, 25, 46, 47) and "The Adoration of the Magi" (22, 23, 44, 45). In the course of his uncommonly creative period of production Bosch painted nine large triptychs which, as a result of their origins, are relatively large and can be traced back to medieval altar-pieces with side-wings. In numerous churches these outsized cupboard-like works can be found which until that time had served almost exclusively the depiction of sacred and traditional themes. Depending on the day and the religious feast, the large wings will either be open (Easter, Christmas etc.) or shut. On the outside of the shutters saints or life-sized patrons are depicted.

Bosch takes this genre and alters little by little its significance and content. He is one of the first to take the form of the triptych and employ it to present unaccustomed themes in new form. Therein lies surely a part of his unfathomable genius which even today presents us with many puzzles. On the other hand, what he opens to our eyes can be thoroughly familiar to us for these are fears and dream-like visions which recur and unsettle us. The paintings take from us parts of these dreary fears.

The theme of the Last Day is, as already stated, treated in the widest sense by the triptychs "The Hay Wain" and "The Garden of Earthly Delights" too, with the result that having first examined the historical development of this genre, we should briefly consider the various groups of triptychs. In the first group the resurrection of the flesh is depicted, in the second the struggle between angelic and demonic creatures for the soul of man against a background of a valley (Vale of Tears). Unfortunately, nothing remains of these works but drawings and later copies. The third group is characterized by the fact that the action takes place in nocturnal landscapes. The bridge across the river recalls Hades, the ruins of the burning town possibly the destruction of Babylon. At the centre of the dramatic situation, the damned suffer terrible tortures, abused by unusual implements. The last group of triptychs include those in which the central compartment features the "Last Day", be it in the form of the Hay Wain scene or the Garden of Earthly Delights. The action in all of these masterpieces is presented as a narrative and can be viewed as a drama in three acts; interestingly, numerous elements in these stories can be traced back to medieval literary notions, but also to illustrations in bibles, bestiaries and other written materials well-known at that time. Alongside the explanation and moral indictment of Bosch's central image appears the depiction of the natural and pre-planned decline of the world in general – a motif which in other areas is described by means of symbols of Vanity (death's head, sand-glass), as in the work of Dürer.

On both outside shutters of the Viennese "Last Day", St Jacob of Compostela and St Bavo of Ghent are depicted in chiaroscuro style (not illustrated). On the left wing Bosch has painted the Fall of the Rebel Angels, the creation of Eve and Original Sin (38), on the right wing the earth itself has become hell; the unavoidable consequences of this process are being decided in the large central compartment of the triptych, the actual "Last Day" (38).

Upon closer inspection it becomes clear that no court scene in the traditional sense is depicted in the central compartment of the "Last Day". God, the judge of the world, surrounded by angels in the upper portion of the painting, does not divide the people into the Good and the Bad, but rather condemns the whole of mankind at a stroke with a wave of his hand; their fate had already been sealed by the Original Sin depicted in the left wing. Even if the portrayal of God the Father on a throne in front of the sun (a symbol of Christ), like that of the arch-angels and saints, corresponds to the canon of prescribed forms in operation since the 11th century, Bosch departs decidedly in the lower part of the painting from the received tradition. With the exception of the angels and saints, only condemned individuals are to be seen in this painting, and they are in the majority after the court session. By omitting the blessed departed, Bosch tells in principle the same story as his numerous predecessors; he remains faithful to the Bible and cannot be dismissed as a heretic. New is his very personal interpretation of the result of the trial: his indictment of major sins, of the vices and failings of mankind, which he explores in his other works too, finds here its most pessimistic and most radical interpretation. The real world and hell come closer together in the painting, are almost united, and even paradise seems paltry, indeed wretched. It seems to us to be worthy of note that Bosch, on the one hand, condemns violence, torture, and hatred in his presentation, yet, on the other hand, explores these vices artistically but at incredible length in these triptychs. It has long been the case that man, despite his fear of hell, has identified more with it than with the comparatively boring paradise which could never capture his imagination in the same way. Do we see here the joys of violence, later discovered by

Sigmund Freud, lived out within the framework of the picture, and thus, too, within the spectator? The eye passes over and takes enjoyment in the individual chaotic scenes which arouse the viewer. Therein lies surely one of the reasons for the overwhelming success of Bosch, and it is no coincidence that kings and princes took pains to receive his pictures, with the result that Bosch soon rose to become a successful artist. With the aid of his universal imagination on the one hand, and his clear artistic integrity on the other, he expressed/painted matters which many people could imagine in their dreams and fantasies but did not dare to make known in public. Who, let's be honest, has not wished at least once in his life tortures similar to those portrayed so impressively by Bosch on a fellow human being? "May you roast in hell..." and other such familiar sayings justify this suspicion. Possibly one lives out such hatred, such fantasies and such deep desires within the framework of the painting (of course!) because they cannot be translated into action in reality. Had Bosch explored subconsciously the principles of sublimation and repression? All these questions remain unanswered in the end but they allow the spectator the chance to find his own personal approach to the painting, and to enter a dialogue with Bosch and the picture. A further interpretation of the scenes of draconian punishment and torture illustrated here, in tandem with an unprecedented concrete imagination, causes us to recall fairytales and other stories from our childhood which develop in literary fashion those images drawn by Bosch. Once again it should be stressed that Bosch's world of images had already existed in the Romanesque period. Distorted faces, grotesque imaginary figures, half animal, plant or human, and caricatured modes of presentation can be found too on Romanesque portals, in older manuscripts and paintings. It would seem that the artist took all these familiar notions, varied and expanded them, and depicted them all together in a manner which in its radicalism was completely new.

The former subjects of miracle plays, theatre performances and other festivals in the Middle Ages – which we can hardly begin to imagine, by the way – are treated here in a fashion reminiscent of film. Bosch's paintings anticipate, as least in part, the horror films and horrific visions of today's society which recently have been portrayed in very realistic fashion in the relevant films. His painting methods have a filmic quality too: his pictures, unlike the great works of the Italian Renaissance, consist of many separate motifs – scenes or miniatures – which we at first see as a whole. Soon, however, the spectator finds himself examining the individual scenes slowly, with a shudder or even pleasure, before these then lead to an overall impression. The artist's technique compels us in the end to tackle the painting step by step, to move from one scene to the next; the view from near and afar is always united.

This can be seen too, of course, in the painting technique. Almost all the shapes and forms are applied in the same colour value, like splashes of colour; they are thus part of the whole and do not stand out from the ground, just as is the case with the central perspective of the Italians. If we have the impression with the Italians that the large figures might at any moment step out of the picture and speak to us (Raphael, Michelangelo), Bosch's figures remain part of the picture surface. By means of such use of colour, perfected by Pieter Breughel the Older, Bosch achieves the impression of a terrible swarming chaos.

That this was an artistic strategy is underlined by the fact that the artist was of course capable of consistent thinking in terms of perspective. He sees the space presented in his picture from the bird's eye view, and it appears that he was certainly acquainted with the new techniques of presentation at that time. This phenomenon is seen more clearly in the painting "The Garden of Earthly Delights" (26, 48–53) or in the second "Last Day" (20, 21, 42, 43). Before the eyes of the spectator the whole world such as it was known at that

time presents itself. But Bosch, the genius, takes back this suggestion of a scheme of the universe immediately, he being a cartographer and discoverer, and casts the spectator's eye into an unspeakable chaos. Bosch's presentation of space and colour shows him to command two incredibly artistic techniques which he varies with unprecedented skill. His triptychs, in this case "The Last Day", also recall Albrecht Altdorfer (1480–1538), who in his "Battle of Alexander at Issus" likewise applies those visions of space so typical of the "Age of Discovery".

When looking at "The Last Day", as at other paintings by Bosch too, we cannot avoid not just general astonishment at his expertise but also the stimulation of our other senses – in our minds, of course. Such "appetizers", the stimulation of all our senses, would seem to be an additional master-stroke. Large pots are bubbling wherever you look, you can smell the most unusual odours, you can hear knives being sharpened, the screams of the tortured, and the hellish noise of the witches' kitchens (40). In other places we grope at slippery lizard and fish fragments on human beings and animals, and are pierced and tortured by thorns, spears and sharp knives (39). Hieronymus Bosch unfolds a raging orgy of gruesome proportions and in doing so appeals to the senses to such an extent that the spectator could fall faint or even into a trance as a result of his indignation and his concealed desire. A drama is staged here which in many ways makes excessive demands on our "handicapped" imagination. In this raging chaos a separate fate overwhelms each tormented victim, each scene differs from the next, and above it all stand the angels, the saints, and God. The artist leaves us to wonder how such a massacre could arise: that is the irony of the story, or Bosch's irony, or the will of God.

In the painting almost all known vices come together and present fatal qualities to the eyes of the spectator in drastic fashion. But not only vice preys on the victims, the devil too, as in real life, has many faces and forms; for example, he becomes strange combinations of parts of lizards and snake-heads with spikey extremities, or of rats, mice and the bodies of insects. It is as if evolution were abolished, the parts remixed and developed further in a chaotic manner – a vision which inspires fear everywhere today too in view of genetic engineering. The destructive diseases rampant at that time such as the plague and leprosy, which led to mutilation and are here drawn in exaggerated manner and in all possible variations, represented a growing catastrophe. The whole of Europe trembled at that time in the face of such uncheckable diseases which swept away the population of entire towns, and it is almost certain that the exposure to fears of this kind led to the imaginative world which Bosch depicts, although at that time such diseases were traced back to the evilness of mankind. People saw the plague and the announcements of Bosch that hell had become bitter reality even in their lifetimes as the punishment of God. With his assimilation of the central compartment and the right wing – earth and hell – Bosch proceeds accordingly; he cannot refrain from building into his pictures a certain irony and naivety. In this way he denies them too clear and too serious a message and thus makes the works bearable for us; hell cannot be as bad as it appears in these visions, the spectator will conclude. God himself offers in this picture the possibility of enduring this inferno as a temporary condition by warning man to live according to Christian virtues. "Good news is no news", however, and so the "bad news" portrayed claims our undivided attention; this is the case too in this "Last Day" in which, surely, our eyes will linger only briefly on the left wing, on paradise.

20, 21, 42, 43 The Last Day (Last Judgement). Oil on panel, central compartment 99.2 x 60.5 cm; wings 99.5 x 28.8 cm. Bruges, Musée Communal des Beaux Arts

This work is significantly smaller than the "Last Day" in

Vienna (38–41) and therefore makes quite different demands on the artist who must restrict himself to fewer details than were possible in the other large triptychs. Nevertheless the task and the development of both the theme and the presentation are executed in masterly fashion.
On the outside shutters of both wings a "Mocking of Christ" by the Master has recently been uncovered. The central compartment shows in accustomed manner the "Last Day" (20), the left wing depicts paradise (42, 43), and the right earth which once again has become hell. The composition of this "Last Day" is comparable to that of the Viennese painting. From the gloriole Christ shows us his wounds. In the traditional manner of the Middle Ages Christ is depicted here as a ruler on his throne, just as the evangeliar states. Around God the King gather trombone-playing angels and ecstatic saints. Dark clouds of smoke fill the wide sky and so make this dignified scene seem all the more removed. At the transition from sky to earth can be seen a Netherlandish seascape and a blazing harbour town. The inferno in the town is all the more effective for being presented as a nocturnal scene, an inferno familiar to those of us today who experienced the destructive nocturnal bomb raids of World War Two. The punishing lightning transforms town and landscape into a bizarre and lambent sea of flames.
Two thirds of the picture are dedicated to the description and interpretation of the result of the "Last Day", and it is once again striking that Bosch does not focus at all on the court scene. Bosch has anticipated the outcome; he changes the action at the expense of those expelled by God who are exposed to every thinkable torture. For Bosch, most men are evil and he dismisses them a priori to hell. He allows only a chosen few the tranquillity and blissful peace of paradise on the left wing. This paradise is quickly forgotten once again, however, as the spectator's gaze drifts on inevitably to the description of hell and earth. Amid the inferno we see two heavy millstones pulled by two fat, naked creatures. The stones crush a victim who makes a last hopeless attempt to escape torture. To the left of that, Bosch has tied a further condemned man to a harp, the target of an arboreal monster. At other points, demons roast human beings above crackling fires, sinners are gulped down by witches and quartered or ill-treated in cages and pots. In a piece of distillery apparatus topped by a baldachin we recognize the naked clergy, a bishop with a mitre, nuns and other priests (21). They have congregated to play an obscure game, and the toad on the round table marks them as the devil's people. Soon the doors of their little "house" will be closed and the fire beneath it lit. All levels of society share the same fate of hellish tortures, and the crew of the escaping ship is the victim of a giant whale.
Although, in this picture, hardly imaginable tortures are enacted, these were not figments of the imagination of man at that time but bitter reality. No age has known as many terrible variations on methods of punishment as the Middle Ages. Torture chambers in museums, descriptions of the burning of witches, and penal codes of the period bear eloquent witness even today to this epoch. Bosch knew these draconian excesses and documented them in his paintings for posterity. But here we find not just a lexicographical list of torture methods both known and still to be invented, but also of all those innovations available to the aspiring science of alchemy. The 15th century was an epoch of unthought-of discoveries and inventions. The view of the world, static until then, and coined by the strong institutions of the Church and the powers of the State, underwent dissolution and upheaval. Revolutions, reformations, and new scientific insights made the worldly and the more spiritual feel uncertain and fearful. Bosch goes as far in his experimental depictions as to suggest sometimes that the expected results of industrious research represent the work of the devil. Is it perhaps a fear of similar origin which nudges us and our painters towards feared visions of horror in view of nuclear dangers?

A maze of allegories, symbols and illusions, complicated, interlaced, and thus difficult to interpret, predominate in the depiction of paradise (42, 43). On a superficial level, we recognize once again a Netherlandish landscape in the central compartment. Without an obvious goal, a ship makes its way through bluey-green floods. Beneath the open pink baldachin naked figures await bliss. Choirs of angels watch over the artistically draped boat. Bosch hints not only at the amusement of paradise which possibly even appears banal, but also at the journey of these souls to their deserved refuge. The strange tower construction is an imaginative cross between a tower, a small Gothic spire, a reliquary and a fountain, decorated with glass jewels. One possible, indeed the best-known, interpretation points to the fountain of youth which promises not just life but eternal good health. Constant cleansing throughout one's life means that one's soul can rise gradually to God, to whom the architectural design of the fountain also points. The fountain reveals echoes of Gothic cathedrals which were conceived as the house and town of God. The devil's town on earth, on the other hand, is painted on the right wing and shows a torture tower.

19 The Descent of the Damned into Hell, Hell, The Earthly Paradise, The Ascent into the Heavenly Paradise

Oil on panel, 86.5 x 39.5 cm (all four paintings). Venice, Palazzo Ducale
These four paintings, too, were once part of a large triptych which was to depict the "Last Day". It is thus the fourth time that Bosch tackles this penetrating theme; unfortunately only these four wings are still extant. According to information passed down, two panels joined to become one wing of the whole triptych, such that Paradise in Heaven and on Earth was depicted on the left, and the Fall of the Damned to Hell on the right. Unlike the other portrayals of the "Last Day", this work, we can assume, found use in a church; for this reason Bosch opted not to present his demonic world. As regards the treatment of the theme, Bosch adheres on the whole to traditional prescribed motifs; and yet in his pictorial expression of these great truths he goes further than had ever been known before. He creates completely new links in terms of space and meaning which connect with the imagined world of famous mystics and which had never been painted in this way.
The "Ascent into the Heavenly Paradise" is without doubt the most radical new portrayal of this theme in pictorial art. Again and again critics have simplified matters by suggesting that the comparable visons of Salvador Dali can be traced back to Bosch. This can be seen clearly in the pictures which share the same title: "The Temptation of St Anthony" (24, 25, 46, 47). Although comparable basic moods can be detected in the visionary imaginations of both artists, they are completely independent artistic personalities. No doubt Dali attempts to express in his paintings those fears of our times which certainly troubled Bosch and his contemporaries too, but man at that time was much more deeply rooted in tradition, in the power of the State, and in the Church, than is the case today.
Dazzled by light from beyond this world, dazzled by the magic and strength derived from this source of God-given light, these human creatures in Bosch's painting free themselves from the Vale of Tears on earth. As though in a trance they fly upwards, released from gravity, towards the light. At the end of this tunnel, which is flooded with light and which hypnotizes the spectator, the true light, paradise and God can be discerned. It is the same effect as that employed nowadays by modern science (hypnosis, trance) to lead man into "another world". While dazzled, we become, as in normal life too, blind for a short moment and consequently incapable of action. For the world around us we seem strange while hypnotized, but we give those around us the chance to penetrate deeply into our innermost thoughts and feelings, just as here the people, in their trance-like state, rise gradually, indeed are even sucked upwards by the God-given light and by truth. Overwhelmed by happiness, they are led in their helplessness by angels up to the tunnel through which they have then to wander.
In keeping with literary models, this tunnel is divided into various sections in which the soul is cleansed and the individual enlightened, and so the happy spirits, drunk with sleep, stagger through space, out into the universe, towards God. There is, as is usual in Bosch's work, an important transition from a naturalistic to a fantastic and allegorical landscape which the artist portrays impressively. This talent of Bosch, who is at the height of his career, is unique and distinguishes him both from his predecessors and from his successors. He may present his figures in the lower part of the four wings in a realistic landscape, in this case paradise, but he develops the landscape little by little to create a magical and imaginative setting; we cannot resist its effect.

22, 23, 44, 45 The Adoration of the Magi

Oil on panel, 138 x 72 cm; wings 138 x 33 cm. Madrid, Prado
"The Adoration of the Magi", i.e. the adoration of the Three Wise Men and the bringing of the gifts on the Epiphany, is the subject of another large triptych, a genre which appealed particularly to Bosch since it placed him in a position to link together interesting situations, stories, and above all levels of meaning. Bosch gave this medieval genre a new significance, new subjects. In this work too, he takes a traditional event, and dresses it in traditional forms, but in the course of his interpretation he goes way beyond the actual story, as is revealed by an analysis of the at first concealed images and symbols. Western Christian traditions, knowledge of the Bible, and habit cause us to think immediately of the Wise Men when we see this painting, and a misinterpretation of the scene can initially be avoided. In the case of "The Vagabond" (59) a larger number of possible interpretations seems imaginable. Nonetheless, Bosch had hidden a whole array of related symbols and allegories in "The Adoration of the Magi" which we must decode. First, however, we wish to perceive and explain what is "visible"; those meanings which are not readily understandable are extremely complex and inter-related, like those similarly mixed-up and even today still incomprehensible associations of ideas which characterize the other great triptychs. Against the background (22) can be seen a tumble-down hut; beneath its ruined penthouse Mary sits in rich gowns, the Infant Jesus in her lap, and she receives the gifts of the Wise Men (23). The men stand before the timber-framed hut, magnificently dressed in garb fit for kings, and they kneel or adopt a reverential position before the Redeemer.
In and behind the hut, as on its straw roof, we recognize strange shepherd-like figures who attend the venerable scene with scepticism. The contrast between the ruined hut, the poor figures, the barren landscape, and the rich kings seems odd too, but it is consciously selected and has nothing whatsoever to do with the traditional romantic depictions of this theme. Another contrast to other triptychs by Bosch should be noted, for he has the task here of concentrating the attention of the spectator solely on the important experience of the Epiphany. On each of the three panels the same action is depicted; it is one scene in three pictures. In this way the depiction becomes monumental. In this way too, however, the internal contradiction of the action is monumentalized; the appearance of the Lord is positive, but the interpretation built in by Bosch is negative. And so we have reached the contradiction inherent in this story, a contradiction further underlined by the fantastic architecture in the background.
From the door of the stable a weird figure looks sneeringly across to the adoration (44). It is half-naked, wears a robe and a crown. This figure, ambiguous in terms of physiognomy and character, represents a

parody and at the same time a mockery of the suffering Christ, and so of that condition which lies at the end of the path of the Redeemer, of that Redeemer who here still rests as a child in his mother's lap. Without doubt this man provides a puzzle. It is an incarnation of the Antichrist which Bosch offers here: the Antichrist as a symbol of evil, his body disfigured by leprosy, which recalls Christ's disfigurement when he is tortured, just as this figure's crown is reminiscent of the crown of thorns. If, on grounds of his appearance, we regard this man as a demonic Antichrist, and if we view him together with the in part Babylonian architecture in the background, then we must conclude that there has never been such a daring and ambiguously pessimistic treatment of the Epiphany in the history of painting. Bosch risks this unprecedented pictorial interpretation of a traditional theme for the first time, and hands over to us, alongside the explicable, a whole series of puzzles yet to be solved. One interpretation of this devilish figure goes as far as to regard it as the Jewish Messiah. The Messiah is present, but unnoticed, with his followers at the birth of Christ and embodies, so to speak, the antitype of the Christian God. Jesus came into the world completely unexpectedly and in a form other than that expected by the Jews. Christ was thus not a Messiah in the sense of the traditional expectations. This interpretation is no longer doubted nowadays; but hotly disputed are the interpretations of the table as a synagogue soon to collapse, of the donkey as a Jewish graven image, and of the Antichrist as a high priest of the synagogue. Of course, one could take the interpretation so far as to perceive in the painting the opposition between the traditional Church and the Reformation, in which case the obscure figures would represent incarnations of the evil and belligerent Church. We cannot escape the fact that Bosch, in many of his paintings, portrays the clergy again and again as personifications of evil and vice. The complexity of the levels of meaning immanent in this painting is reflected in a further interpretation which does not exclude the first. It appears that the Epiphany can be seen here, but in fact, on a symbolic and allegorical level, the Eucharist is depicted, i.e. a sacrament is made visible. Mary, seated, should be seen as an altar on which the body of Christ appears, as in the Eucharist. Balthazar is the priest who kneels before the altar and throne and co-celebrates the Mass with Melchior and Caspar. In disguised fashion, Bosch presents before our eyes the eternal repetition of Christ's return to earth. The images on Melchior's cloak illustrate, as well as the sacrifice of Manoa, the visit by the Queen of Sheba to King Solomon, and thus constitute a typological reference to the Adoration of the Magi. On the orb (45) which Caspar hands over to Christ, a heathen scene is depicted: the pelican recalls Christ's sacrifice on the cross and his salvation. On the helmet at one king's feet we recognize a further allegory: the sacrifice of Isaac points forward to the sacrificial death of the Redeemer, although in this context hints at sensual pleasure might be noted. The traditional scenes from the Old and New Testaments depicted here, such as they are combined with a portrayal of vice and sin, represent in this way an invention of Bosch, who was not only in a position to recognize and comprehend these complicated connections, but also to illustrate them in a binding manner. The ambiguity of the various levels of meaning is handled in truly masterly fashion, and only the spectator capable of "reading" and of understanding can not only absorb the superficial and recognizable message of the painting but also come to certain conclusions. Bosch illustrates such matters superbly and, on the other hand, defends himself against possible attacks from the authorities by depicting traditional elements too. Just as in the story about the Emperor's new clothes, he nodded in acknowledgement with everybody else, but he maintained silence in public about the nakedness of his revelations since he could assume that everyone must recognize the obvious. The human greatness of the Master lies without doubt in this intellectual capacity for mimicry.

Bosch proceeds analagously when he fashions the landscape in the background of "The Adoration of the Magi". He interweaves accustomed and fantastic/allegorical elements to such an extent that at first sight only the impression of a town is won, of decorative scenery which has hardly anything in common with the actual action. Noteworthy is the change of perspective which does not strike the spectator since it is so skilfully selected. The artist changes from a front view to an oblique bird's eye view, before then moving over in the background to a parallel front view once again. We know this technique from the foreshortened bird's eye views offered in tourist survey maps nowadays. If we now concentrate on the survey intended here, we see that, strictly speaking, the town is part of this plastic map which Bosch wishes to show us. Of course, he is not interested in the realistic portrayal of a coastal landscape which is here illustrated in curious fashion, but in the depiction of a landscape which helps interpret the remainder of the painting. That is, the landscape has the sole task of elucidating the action in the foreground, of underlining it, and of presenting the internal oppositions discussed above by means of stylistic variation. The far-reaching town is Bethlehem, Jerusalem and Rome in one, cities which, in terms of their fate, can be seen together with Babylon. Reality and vision combine to form a thoroughly credible view. In our memory, and in our daily dealings, we find comfort in the sight of these and similar cities; we are deeply familiar with such romantic sketches. Hardly anyone takes the trouble, however, to examine Bosch's town more closely. Soon we perceive that architectural fantasies are illustrated here, which did not exist then and do not exist today, which for technical reasons could not be built. We see here masterly variations on the theme of circular buildings which could emerge from the vision of today's architects. Imagination, like art, has a double-root: firstly, a liking for games, for playing, a child-like pleasure in experimentation and experience; secondly, an illusion but with meaningful content. These architectural products represent the Babylonian muddle of nations, and thus the world in general; but also the Christian-Jewish Jerusalem that will return on the "Last Day"; and a caricature of the Eternal City of Rome which is a symbol of power, splendour, and justice. So Bosch created in the background of his everyday Eucharist a notion, as comprehensive as it is eternal, of the city as a symbol of the universe. This universal interpretation of the triptych could be trivialized, were this splendid work to be approached improperly. Nothing would remain but a trashy fragment called "Three Wise Men" which would decorate barren rooms in the form of cheap postcards. On the left and right wings, wealthy citizens in rich robes are depicted who attend the holy scene (22). The coats of arms point to both the patrons who commissioned the painting.

24, 25, 46, 47 The Temptation of St Anthony

Oil on panel, 131.5 x 119 cm; wings 131.5 x 53 cm. Lisbon, Museu Nazional de Arte Antiga

This splendid painting by Bosch is, like many paintings of the lives of the saints, also an allegory, with reference here to the life of Anthony (250–356 A.D.). At the centre of the action the artist portrays not just the saint, but above all man, with all his bodily weaknesses, worries and fears, who is to be distracted from his virtuous works by a devilish being. Bosch sees in these Christian models not so much the legendary Saint who has already found his place in heaven; rather he portrays in an impressive and dramatic manner the path of the saint, a path between virtue and vice. The portrayal of the stony path to heaven thus departs in many ways from traditional medieval depictions of the lives of the saints, for these usually show the saint already in heaven with few allusions to his earthly existence and tortures.

Illustrated here is not an historical event in the life of St Anthony, but the sum of the possible temptations which tormented him in his lifetime. As a result, the grotesque and curious figures which have congregated in the picture do not represent real or actual protagonists, but personifications of the ideas which troubled St Anthony. Bosch illustrates the thoughts, fears, hopes, but also the hidden vices too, to which Anthony was exposed. Bosch paints the dream-world of the saint, employing an imagination which has provided work for generations of art historians. Alongside the depiction of a landscape Bosch again includes architectural fragments, architectural scenery, and weird crosses between animals, nature and human beings, as well as a series of scenes from various perspectives which in reality would never have been possible. Bosch abolishes gravity and evolution and fashions the visible world, i.e. the dream world, according to his own laws. Even though we have the initial impression that the composition of the picture mirrors an inner order, we soon realize, upon closer inspection, that the world is standing on its head and functioning according to new rules. At this point, of course, we descend into the many and various levels of meaning, such that it is not easy, if actually possible, to decode these allegories.

On the whole, Bosch introduces us to a mad, upside-down world inhabited by devils and demons. Blind to Christian teaching, man and his world have strayed from the right path, have stumbled and fallen prey to heresy. Consequently, we see as the central theme of the central compartment of the triptych (25) the witches' sabbath and the Black Mass, which is celebrated by a bird-like demon beneath the architectural surround (the altar) (47). Both "inner pictures" of the saint, the witches' sabbath and the Black Mass were depicted in this way for the first time in the history of pictorial art, thus reflecting a richly imaginative and inventive mind which exceeds the wildest notions of the world at that time and even today. Moreover, allegories of sensual pleasure, social satire and other vices come together in this painting (24). In the right wing we recognize a woman bathing in the nude and a mussel, both clear references to eroticism and sexual pleasure intended to tempt the saint. The illustrious lady is possibly even a successor of Venus who, born from a mussel, is a symbol of fertility and femininity in general. Bosch sees the woman not as a familiar allegory of beauty and fruitfulness as in the works of Botticelli, but as a devil woman who is to lead the saint into temptation. Anthony who has perceived the set table on the one hand and the tempting "Venus" on the other, turns his head from one scene to the other, to the set table. Bosch offers the holy man no alternative whatsoever; both scenes within his view represent vice-ridden temptations. True, Anthony has opened the Book of Wisdom and attempts to read it; but he does not appear to succeed, for his eyes still turn to the table which is carried, into the bargain, by naked playfellows.

An additional explanation of the left wing is made possible by the quotation of a literary source to which the painting might be traced back. In the "Vitae Patrum" we read that Anthony reached a river at which the devil awaited him in the form of a beautiful woman (see above), of a queen with other beautiful women. At first he did not see through the temptations represented by the bathing women, and he followed them into their town, which appears in the background of the painting. When the queen revealed herself to be a frivolous wench, he grasped his error and fled from the magnificent city. On the left wing of the triptych we become aware of the most well-known temptation of St Anthony. Macabre insect-like demons tear the saint away from the ground and carry him off towards the sky. Soon thereafter Anthony crashes back to earth. A few fellow journeymen discover him, dressed in dark robes, and carry him in his still confused state across the bridge (24).

All three pictures on this great triptych can be traced back to literary sources which Bosch expands according to his own notions. Included among the most significant literary sources, which other contemporary painters have used too, are the aforementioned "Vitae

Patrum", published in Dutch translation under the title "Vaderboeck". The most important written sources were without doubt the "Legenda Aurea", translated into Dutch in 1478, and the version of the life of St Anthony of Athanasius published in 1490. An interesting aspect of this translation of the life of a saint is how the edifying facts are gradually abandoned in favour of more adventurous interpretations. Although the curious details appear to predominate, Bosch manages to balance both aspects of the treatment. Although we are talking about the life of a saint, it can be observed that the more adventurous treatments of this theme have become more numerous in the course of the centuries, for the temptations of St Anthony prove to be one of the most popular themes for artists. In more recent times we have had the surrealistic picture by Dali which in similarly radical fashion treats of the temptations of St Anthony.

Of course, one could get lost among the many details of the triptych and try to measure the symbolic and allegorical value of each one. This exercise might prove successful in separate areas; in others we are reduced to speculations, for Bosch did not provide a description of his paintings, nor are other exact literary sources on the subject known to us. The symbols are of interest only within the overall context, within the system of allegories discussed here. They fit together like the stones in a mosaic, like the pieces of a jigsaw puzzle. One change can alter the meaning of the whole. Thanks to his education, Bosch was conscious of these mysteries, and perhaps he even intended to confuse and unsettle his spectators. Just as Bosch uses his images to stage a mad and upside-down world, so he employs his symbols to construct such mysteries. The result of this process is not just the realization that something is not quite right about the painting; the spectator is forced to take a personal viewpoint on this world. Despite all the arts of interpretation employed, the mystery continues, but not now within the framework of the painting, but within the spectator. In this way Bosch once more displays his unprecedented masterly skills, and perhaps it is this fact which has made him so popular throughout the centuries.

This great art is continued unambiguously at the centre of the triptych, where we recognize the head of St Anthony. Unlike the other demons and devilish figures, he is the only person to look in our direction. With one hand he points to Christ, who can be seen at the rear of the altar in the niche. Both Christ and Anthony have a hand raised as though in a blessing. Jesus points to the crucifix on the altar, and thus to his coming Passion, to his bitter path to the cross. Absorbed in their quiet dialogue, the two seem to inhabit a world of their own which stands in sharp contrast to their environment. Matters relating to alchemy and astrology, notions of heresy, a witch cult, magic, and lechery surround the now shaking intellectual world of Anthony, and only Christ can show him the true way through his faith. As a result of sin and these vice-ridden temptations, the world changes into a Satanic chaos. God's punishment transforms the world into a thundering inferno and evolution-gone-haywire. Man, animals, and nature know no limits. Everything intermingles, everything is possible. Frightening visions of God's creation gone wrong overpower first our thoughts and then the world. Bosch's world has broken up into its separate atoms, and, simultaneously, these smallest parts have come together again in disorganized fashion because the greater will, God's creative energies, are now missing. The costume of the seductive queen (25) becomes a monster's tale; beggars, the poor and crippled turn into demons; the noble knight grows a pig's head. Humans and animals develop monstrous crevices from which crawl new and weird beings. Blood spills from the side of a supposed high priest while he turns into a pig as he celebrates Holy Mass. The figure beneath the architectural surround is assisted by a sacristan who has long lost his human identity. A filter worn as a hat shows that no wisdom can now seep into his consciousness. He is stupid and punished for this foolishness. His cat-like

face, his insect's ears, and his bird-like neighbour have nothing to do with humanity, with truth. The lute-players accompanying this mass opposite the priest hardly produce heavenly tones: his face has turned into the head of a dead horse. He is riding on a plucked goose which searches the barren ground for nourishment. Terrible tones accompany the danse macabre.

Although Bosch entitles the picture "The Temptation of St Anthony", further contemplation would suggest that it revolves round not only his temptations, but also around the desires aroused in the spectator by the painting. Bosch alludes to our hidden vices and yearnings. With a hunger for knowledge and a stunted imagination we consider the uncanny scenes in the painting. We are led into temptation, invited to surrender to the vices portrayed, to change our natures, to put on masks and do things in disguise which are forbidden in our monotonous daily lives. Who would not like to spend time in the "Garden of Earthly Delights", would not like to surrender to gluttony and lust in a paradisiacal landscape? Who would not, from time to time, wish such transformations on his enemies, and who would not savour the joys of torture presented here? Having felt pity for the saint, and having hoped that he might resist the temptations, we find that despite our sanctimoniousness we are long since embroiled in similar temptations. In this way this splendid painting ceases to remain just an artistic depiction of the temptations of the saint and becomes a moral mirror for the spectator.

Finally, we can regard the drama which takes place here as a carnival. Disguised behind all kinds of weird and wonderful masks, the spectator can delve into a new world, once he has acquainted himself with the theme of the carnival. Behind such masks we can yield to our various temptations and inner passions – which is not always advisable in real life. Bosch offers us the possibility of delving deep into ourselves and into the painting, with the guarantee that, afterwards, we can return safely to the path of virtue. Whether this is the path of Christian teaching remains an unanswered question, for Bosch was aware of the need of the Church to be reformed. As in many other paintings by this artist, all social classes are brought together in this triptych. Everyone, the clergy too, is part of this world and exposed to temptations like those faced by St Anthony. That this insight leads us into deeper and deeper allegorical levels is self-evident, and the deeper, the further such interpretations lead, the more complex our explanations become.

In the background of the central compartment, powerful architectural fantasies present themselves to our eyes, burning towns and fragments of buildings apparently knocked together without rhyme or reason and which stretch across the centre and foreground of the painting. Here too we recognize the boundless imagination of the Master, and yet we cannot refrain from suspecting that symbols are hidden behind this dream-like scenery. If we look back to other depictions of towns in pictorial art, we establish that the town has almost always functioned as a symbol of law and order. Within the town walls Christian and worldly powers governed an ordered existence which aimed for a new, paradisiacal Jerusalem. Bosch now alters this picture to the disadvantage to town allegories and makes a place of chaos out of the refuge of harmony. Demonic powers seize possession of the town and cast it into misery and anarchy. Punished by God, those constructions in which demons are at work are cast away to the devil. The town is unmasked as a ruinous area. The architectural fragments shown here point to past magnificence. This splendour is now linked with the equally perishable magnificence of superficial vices such as pomposity, gluttony and lust. From the grotto in which we see the altar and Christ, the eye drifts to a narrow tower or small pillar. Here, scenes from the Old Testament are illustrated which appear to represent beautiful ceramic art. Ancient cults are presented opposite Christian teaching, and the partly heathen customs as well as the painted architecture

are surrendered to destruction. Bosch cannot refrain, however, from allowing his unprecedented imagination to run free here too. The bridge discernible behind the grotto is not ceramic art; it is constructed of parts of a metal object reminiscent of a knight's armour. It is a building constructed in steel, in iron, which was very much possible at that time.

Beneath the iron bridge construction we see a group of various odd figures wading through the dirty water (46). These are curious knight figures who head for the altar where a black mass is being celebrated. They ride on outsized rodents, and one such animal has turned itself into a jug. On this jug, a symbol of gluttony, but one which also points to the sacrifice of blood in the mass, sits a scarecrow; its head has turned into a prickly thistle. A woman turned fish with a small child in her arms sits on a mouse which is her throne. Whether this is a reference to the sacrifice of the Mass, and so to Mary and to the Passion of Christ, cannot be ascertained. Possibly such themes, baptism too, provided a vehicle for such motifs which were then reinterpreted. Similarly obscure is a group which comes from the left to attend the witches' sabbath and the black mass. Cat- and bird-like demons and devils accompany knights and monks to the setting of the macabre cult ceremony. The enormous skewered bird and the wheel of torture point to the sacrifice of blood in the Mass, and are symbols of violence and gluttony at the same time. The broken wine jug of one demon, as well as the impending blood sacrifices, would seem to hint at a trance-like condition and supernatural powers, but we do not know who is to be sacrificed here. Is it the bird, the lion-like creature, or other beings which will follow this procession? It is only certain that all these groups are heading for the centre of the picture, the altar, and will try to include St Anthony in their frightening games. Whether he will succumb to these temptations and vices is not apparent in the painting. St Anthony is still undecided.

26, 48–53 The Garden of Earthly Delights

Oil on panel, 220 x 195 cm; wings 220 x 97 cm. Madrid, Prado

In this splendid triptych by Bosch, the Master of Imagination develops to become both an actor in, and a director of, a simply incredible universal depiction of the world. In this cycle of pictures Bosch realizes not only his deepest dreams, which are perhaps also part of our dreams, but aspires to the position of "judge" over heaven and hell, just as he did in the portrayals of the Last Day. As such, he is no longer attached to the strictly hierarchical world of the Middle Ages and scholasticism, but now a child of the "unrelenting" Renaissance. This era which begins in about 1450 in Italy, i.e. in the year of the birth of the artist, places in question in radical fashion the medieval view of the world. Just as the figures in Bosch's paintings undergo transformations, so the view of the world of the generations of that period must change. In all areas of politics, art, science and religion, far-reaching changes take effect with the goal of trying to attain a new view of the world. If the Italian Renaissance begins initially to query and change man's view of the world, its new discoveries represent horror visions for Bosch. These changes – the discovery of other continents, the exploration of the universe by physicists and astronomers, and the new revolutionary advances of medicine and chemistry – give rise to hopes on the one hand, but add fuel to unanticipated fears on the other. Just as nowadays people tend to be pleased about new advances, but a fear, not to be underestimated, remains about the danger of progress.

Bosch, living at the point of intersection of these two epochs, tackles these hopes and fears more clearly than ever in his "Garden of Earthly Delights". Until then, thoughts of paradise, eternal life and the fountain of youth had been associated with such paintings. Bosch dresses this theme in the form of the traditional triptych reserved for the Church, and offers the spectator a new, unprecedented and daring depiction of the "Garden of Earthly Delights». He presents for us an eternal night-mare of mankind and tries to hide this dream in symbols with which we are all deeply familiar. We recognize therein not only an allegorical warning, but also the realization of a few of our long-cherished desires, and our longing for security, eternal life and love. Nevertheless, "The Garden of Earthly Delights" is one of the most disputed paintings by Bosch. Generations of experts have struggled to give an overall account of this work. Many succeeded in finding plausible explanations for parts of the painting; a convincing overall interpretation has yet to be formulated. Does the picture represent a condemnation, a warning against man's sins of the flesh, or a utopia, the ideal picture of peaceful society? Is it a depiction of mankind before the flood, or a demonic picture of the cults of a sect? Sources call the work an illustration of the "variety in the world", and of the path of man from Creation (Paradise) to Hell, to hell on earth. Whereas Bosch's other great triptychs, e.g. the "Last Day", were to be read and interpreted from left to right, from Creation to Hell as the final destination, "The Garden of Earthly Delights" can hardly be interpreted as a cycle, as a path for mankind. Does it possibly represent an ultimate condition, a lasting condition in this life or the next? Is this garden, as a destination, part of hell or of paradise?

All these questions, as already indicated, have not yet found conclusive answers, and the justified question arises: could Bosch not have provoked this uncertainty deliberately? Perhaps there is no answer to this question, perhaps the artist aimed consciously to unsettle his audience. Although Bosch presents a visionary utopia, he himself possibly had no answer to eschatological questions, just as Thomas More depicts a new world in his novel "Utopia" but is himself unsure about the path which leads to it.

It is as impossible to comprehend the omnipotence of God the creator with all its (for us) questionable appearances as it is, in the terms of the biblical parable, to fill a lake into a glass. Surely Bosch is pointing here to the futility of always wishing to explain everything. It is perhaps just as difficult to comprehend the miracle of creation as it is to comprehend what Bosch wished to say with this triptych. We must be content, probably, with the observation that not just "The Garden of Earthly Delights" but also other paintings by the Master are, in the final analysis, not explicable. That does not mean, however, that they lose any of their significance. On the other hand, this mystery leaves many paths open, it stimulates and bewings our imagination, and allows us to experience the painting in a new way each day and to have a quite personal relationship to it. In the left wing, the story of the triptych begins its development, and already we come across several curiosities. The creation of Eve in the heavenly paradise is depicted. God the Father ensouls Eve by giving her his arm, a procedure which we know from Michelangelo's frescos in the Vatican (The Creation of Adam). Here Adam is sitting still drunk with sleep on the green meadow and looks at both God and Eve in astonishment. It is interesting, when comparisons are made with the other triptychs, to note that the expulsion from paradise is omitted. Are the individuals here not affected by the expulsion, do they find themselves in a paradise on earth already? This supposition is permissible, for no judge of the world is to be seen who divides mankind into the Good and the Bad. Whereas Bosch condemns mankind in his portrayals of the "Last Day" to an existence in a hellish inferno, he offers here an alternative interpretation of the Last Day. Thanks to the grace of God all have come to share in paradise. This paradise, the eternal Garden of Eden, finds its apparently uninterrupted continuation in the central compartment (26, 48). Unlike the other triptychs, the transition in the landscape here from the left wing to the central compartment is smooth. A further contrast lies in the fact that in this painting Bosch draws not a landscape familiar to us, e.g. the Netherlandish coast, used again and again, but a garden pleasing to the eye.

Nature develops to become an artificial construction, a staged artificiality, which is so skilfully selected that it itself becomes natural again, and we can discover in the first instance no obvious contrast. It is an exotic paradisiacal garden such as only our imagination can paint. Nature in the actual sense is here an omnium gatherum of known and unknown plants, familiar and unfamiliar animals, as well as individual fantastic architectural fragments. In a few details of the landscape we are reminded of naive painting, and this painting contains without doubt naive details; Bosch may even have consciously included naive elements. It has already been suggested that the imaginative world of the Master not only reveals similarities with naive painters, but especially with the drawings of children. Just as a child exaggerates things, alters their dimensions, subjects proportions to his own laws, and creates fantasy figures which we cannot identify, so Bosch builds these elements into his own paintings and gives them a new, his own, order.

Bosch's knowledge of all possible animals and plants, which were surely not known to the average citizen at that time, is astonishing too. The world portrayed here shows us with almost lexical exactitude an omnium gatherum of the animals and plants known in the 16th century. In this way Bosch shows himself to be an observer and researcher who paid attention to minute detail and who was very well informed about scientific research carried out at that time.

Art and nature intermingle in this painting in an unprecedented manner. Wherever you look, the earth opens up like a volcano, and rocks emerge to become immediately plants or architectural fragments which then bring forth strange buds and blossoms. Plants, animals and architecture mingle, and Bosch's fantastic constructions become identical with evolution in nature, but the artist develops his own laws of evolution which, in this form, are not actually possible. The people who play and live here and apparently take pleasure in their existence, deny interpretation too. Are they in a paradisiacal hell, or in God's paradise, or has the earth itself in the end turned into paradise or hell? We do not know. The manner in which this painting handles nature and evolution, gravity and the laws of nature, results in the presentation of a mad and upside-down universe. The ambiguity of the details means that no overall message can be evaluated, no unambiguous allegorical interpretation is possible. If we examine the details of this splendid painting in greater depth and at greater length, our questions become all the more curious and questionable, all the more unanswerable, for in the end everything is possible in this world. Tomorrow, this picture, which is in a constant state of flux, might look quite different. Bosch takes away from us the certainty of knowing and shows us that we actually know absolutely nothing, for this picture, like the world itself, might be a cunning apparition, a fantastic deception.

The creatures which play their wild games in the central compartment, which, intertwined, indulge in lust and play with fish and birds, are neither angels nor devils, neither good nor evil (49). They are probably sylphs or elemental spirits animated by the four elements. It is a world beyond good and evil, a theme which later crops up in the philosophy of the 19th century. Under the influence of alchemy and the rapid development of the natural sciences, Bosch considers the world here not in terms of good and evil, hell and paradise, but in terms of the independent evolution of the elements. The end of the world would be, in this case, not the "Last Day", but a possible ultimate condition at the end of evolution, of matter in general. Bosch, in defiance of all the principles of natural sciences, took this to absurd lengths. The many flying fish which look partly like transparent embryos, for example, cannot be explained otherwise. Those people and couples who linger in glass balls which look like outsized amniotic sacs remain inexplicable too. Without doubt, Bosch hints at the lust of these naked figures; nevertheless, the interpretation of these details does not lead to an

overall account of the triptych, but rather to an appreciation of the absurdity of the whole work, as described above.

Adam and Eve, whom we readily associate with paradise, become couples who sit close together, hide themselves away, show themselves in public and play with each other. Everybody comes together with everybody else, and so the cheerful atmosphere of this depiction alludes not simply to the vice of lust, but represents an allegory of the self-propagating nature of life, a symbol of the eternal life in nature. Nevertheless, and for that very reason, man is here no longer an individual, a being capable of self-recognition, but rather part of a giant mechanism, a nature-machine which he must obey. Everyone is equal and bound by the same laws. Thus Bosch perceives on the one hand the principle of equality for all, i.e. of a positive teaching, but he immediately accentuates its negative qualities, possibly in the sense of a man like George Orwell. The individual is abandoned in favour of a new unity, a utopia which instils fear in us too. The fantastic and absurd elements of this work correspond to the ambivalent feelings of the spectator. There is a constant shifting between longing and fear, which is further proof that Bosch does not emphasize Good and Evil here but something completely new. The whole painting is an "erotic dream", a "Tausendjähriges Reich" or "a chaotic insoluble puzzle", in the words of a few respected Bosch experts. This puzzle is reflected too in the depiction of the technical constructions and architectural fragments. Exotic fountains of life, metal spheres, glass shapes, kettle constructions, and outsized apparatus from the chemistry laboratory form fixed points and settings in this picture, and they too have no unambiguous function and are open to many and varied interpretations. As regards the interpretation of these conjuring props, as of the shells, eggs and bubbles too, we probably find ourselves confronted in each case with the fact that an explanation is impossible (52, 53).

In the right wing of the triptych (50) hell is depicted. It remains a strange fact that man is here punished for sins which he has not committed in the central compartment and right wing, for in the centre of the painting man lives without birth, death and the ageing process in a time which has no awareness of sin. These people lead a rather cheerful existence, commit sins, but are not aware of these vices, as they are still marked by innocence on the one hand, and obey the laws of nature on the other. To the right of that, Bosch presents to our eyes the flood, i.e. a possible version of hell, in which man is made to suffer; he is helpless and clueless as he is not aware of his sin (51). Satanic and hellish tortures, macabre torture methods and a burning town point unambiguously to the punishment of mankind (52); yet the question of what the reason is for this terrible punishment remains open. If the central compartment points to the position of mankind in Noah's time, then the social classes of this world, depicted in the right wing, have no obvious relationship to the central compartment. The "Garden of Earthly Delights", as a whole, is a depiction of a "utopia for mankind", of a utopia which initially may seem valueless. The right wing with the portrayal of the flood and of hell fetches us out of these dreams without any nonsense, and reminds us that we still live on this earth. In this way, the dream of the "Garden of Earthly Delights" finds its abrupt end, initially at least! In the upper part of hell (52) we see not only a town drowning in flood and flames, but also parts of a torture machine. Wheels which have become ears carry a knife which has developed from a cannon. This slaughter machine makes its way through a sea of sinners to quarter them, a torture method included in the code of medieval punishments. Behind that, poor souls are led to the gallows by devilish figures, via lambent flames. Similarly weird and inhospitable is the alchemistic apparatus next to the "ears-cannon". In this distiller people are boiled or cleansed so that their souls, in purified condition, can commence a new journey; where to remains unclear.

Beneath this scene we recognize pale naked figures in a white shell, an oval container. It appears that this is supposed to hint at a den or joint, for several creatures are gathered around a table and are becoming drunk with great relish. A dignitary of the Church pours wine from a barrel which he will then serve to the group. Even in hell man cannot refrain from yielding to gluttony and intemperance. But new tortures and transformations are already awaiting these spirits given to vice.

27, 28, 29, 54–56   The Hay Wain

Oil on panel, 135 x 100 cm; wings 135 x 45 cm. Madrid, Prado

If the "Garden of Earthly Delights" is a daring depiction of a utopia for mankind, then "The Hay Wain" mirrors human characteristics in a way which corresponds to the deep devoutness of the artist. The "Hay Wain" is, as a whole, a symbol of transience and avarice, but also an allegory for other vices such as gluttony and lust. Bosch has placed the depiction of human interests and vices at the centre of his work; so he seems to moralize and condemn. If we consider the triptych, a second layer of significance becomes clear, however, which shows the "Hay Wain" to be an expansion of the "Last Day". Just like the various versions of "The Last Day" by Bosch, the "Hay Wain" begins in the left wing with the portrayal of paradise (29). The story of paradise can be seen here, as well as the unavoidable consequences for the protagonists. The Fall of the Rebel Angels is followed by the creation of Adam and Eve, which is embedded in a landscape pleasing to the eye, the temptation by the serpent, and, right at the bottom, the expulsion from paradise. In the right wing (29) the history of mankind meets its unhappy end. In hell the sinners do penance in the form of terrible tortures for the errors made in the central compartment.

To this extent this painting does not differ from the "Last Day". In the central compartment Bosch ventures out onto new paths when he replaces the court scene with the depiction of the hay wain (54). In this way he portrays in unambiguous symbols the path of man between paradise and hell, to which the waggon, moving from left to right, points. The hay wain rolls towards its inevitable goal, a place portrayed here as hell, but which is also a place of truth and the final destination of human deceptions. Unlike in medieval depictions of the "Last Day", God is not present in the central compartment of this triptych. Bosch gives his own interpretation which is related to his portrayal of the "Seven Deadly Sins" (64). God is everywhere and sees everything, and for this reason it is not necessary to depict him here. Moreover, Bosch interprets a quotation from the Bible which can be seen as a second reason for God not appearing in person here: in the Bible God indicates that he will hide his face and consider what is to be the end of mankind. Bosch anticipates this fate, for in his opinion man is evil and deserves the place of truth which is hell. Whether man can enter heaven after hell, which can also be purgatory, is left open by Bosch. For the moment punishment awaits man for all those deeds executed in the central compartment.

The hay wain is the world, mankind always on the move, just as was illustrated in the "Garden of Earthly Delights". The wheels, turning and turning, point to the passing of time, and to fate too – think of lottery wheels and the wheels of fortune (55). On the hay wain sits a couple who listen to music, here, like the hay, a symbol of the transience of all that is worldly (Vanity). Human life is like a sound which soon fades away between heaven and hell. The elegantly dressed couple and their companions linger in the central sphere of the painting, are part neither of heaven nor of the actual world which pulls the hay wain, accompanies or follows it. It is a place where nothing has been decided. An angel looks up to God and is the only person in the hay wain procession to see him. To the right of that, a demon or a devil plays on his flute which was once his nose. Music is here intended to be an unambiguous symbol of transience, but the couple and their com-

panions have not yet decided in favour of Good or Evil. The music they listen to could just as well be heavenly tones or diabolical rhythms. In this region which belongs to this world, a mediation between heaven and hell, between truth and falsehood, and between virtue and vice can still take place, a shimmer of hope in a world of sin. Neither the devil nor the angels have won the struggle for the soul of man. Independently of the waggon, the hay can receive its own interpretation which largely goes back to literary sources: "All flesh is grass and all the goodliness thereof is as the flower of the field" (Isaiah), and: "As for man, his days are as grass: as a flower of the field, so he flourisheth" (Psalm 103). So the hay represents sensual pleasures, vices, and the obsession with fame (which passes). The demons which drag this waggon in the direction of hell, represent the various vices of this world (28). People who follow this waggon without thinking, who are occupied only by their own selves and by avarice, who are blind to God, gather all earthly goods which are like grass/hay, for they themselves are as grass: short-lived and perishable. But Bosch does not depict only avarice and rapacity; he shows too other qualities of man which overstep the laws of God. In the foreground we recognize the brutal scene of a murder, to the right of that a fat monk, whose sisters pack the hay into sacks for him. In the centre of the foreground is a scene which resembles "The Cure of Folly". A quack cuts the last remains of reason from the head of a lady and treats her in keeping with her vanity. Perhaps she is undergoing a beauty operation, in order to be even prettier and even more vain, but she does not notice that just the opposite is happening to her. The scene further to the left points to gluttony and vanity too, for there two well-dressed bourgeois ladies praise their own elegance, while behind them a skewer alludes to gluttony.

Behind the waggon can be seen a further scene (27) which in the overall context points to a new layer of significance and a new story. Elegantly dressed rulers ride in leisurely fashion behind the waggon; these are princes, kings and other dignitaries of this world who have nothing to do with the commoners. They follow the hay wain blindly, convinced that they are being admired by the commoners. But these people hardly bother about the distinguished gentlemen and are obsessed with their own fate. In this way Bosch makes the great gentlemen seem ridiculous and as perishable as the citizens who accompany the waggon; these facts reflect without doubt Bosch's abhorrence of such power and pretension. Whereas rulers had been portrayed until then mostly as models who indicated a moral path for the people to follow, the artist degrades the dignitaries in this painting. They are just as foolish and blind as the rest of the population. Their ridiculous behaviour is emphasized by the fact that they do not follow a triumphal car or some other insignia of the ruling State, as was usual until then, but a banal hay wain which, into the bargain, shows them the way to hell. Bosch's cynicism is self-explanatory and borders on the depiction of carnival processions which were very popular at that time. The rulers and their subjects are part of one carnival procession which surrenders itself to ridicule without even realizing it. By means of this common self-deception Bosch does away with any differences between the people and returns to the main message of the painting: all men are as perishable as the plant in the field and as hay. It was clear to Bosch that this represented a very drastic evaluation of society. By masking the world behind the absurd hay wain procession, he protected himself, however, against direct interpretations and thus against attacks by the Inquisition.

This procession can be understood as a perversion of the "Trionfi" common in the 14th and 15th centuries, i.e. of splendid celebratory processions. They were a deeply-rooted tradition in Italy which goes back in part to customs of the antique. The good town government which protected its citizens, won victories for them, and served the people, marched through the town on special occasions and let itself be celebrated. For

weeks on end the communes were decorated by the best artists in order to create an honourable framework for the processions, for after all people were celebrating not just the City Fathers and governors but themselves too. We know a whole series of splendid depictions of these triumphant festival processions from paintings and written sources. Not just the rulers and nobility, the commoners and the soldiers were presented here, but also a picture of the elegant and proud town. The town was always a symbol in these pictures for law and order, beauty and truth, which were symbolized by the government too. Above everything stood God, who blessed and directed the fate of the town. War, diseases, vices and injustice etc. were hardly worthy of depiction, and were banished, if shown at all, to beyond the walls of the town. Outside the town walls, injustice, war and vice prevailed. Bosch discards this interpretation and has the illustrious grouping travel through the land. His hay wain procession is no triumphant procession of a good town government, of virtuous citizens and clergymen, but the complete opposite: unsuspectingly, these perfidious people follow the symbol of transience, the hay, and it appears that this is a procession in which foolishness and vice triumph. We perceive not an ordered procession but a chaos of separate groups which have nothing to do with each other, do not see each other, and get in each other's way. Mercilessly this strange group continues on its way, with no consideration for the individual and his goal. Helplessness soon spreads among them, impotence and confusion accompany man. A few try to climb up ladders onto the waggon, to board it or stop it with the aid of all kinds of instruments, but in vain, it would seem. Others have accepted their fate, they begin to dance, to celebrate, or plunge into apathy and drunkenness.

In sharp contrast to this procession which is depicted in rich bright splashes of colour is a peaceful blue-green landscape which in the background gives way to the delicate and shining light blue of the distant horizon. Whereas the surface in the foreground appears hardly as a landscape but as a barren "wilderness", Bosch conjures up behind the hay wain a natural setting which is the complete opposite. This does not belong to the wild lawless world of the human figures but has its own rhythms. The natural world still displays a sense of order, is beautiful and pleasing to the eye, it obeys only cosmic principles which foolish man cannot influence.

In the composition and technical execution of the landscape Bosch shows himself to be a mature and experienced artist. As a man of the 15th century he commands all the technical possibilities of his age and introduces us to a landscape which belongs to the Modern Era and not any more to the Middle Ages. The perspectival system is worked out to the last detail, and the unity of tone in the background suggests an atmosphere of its own which has little in common with the medieval painting techniques employed in the foreground. The thematic and symbolic contrast between the foreground and background is thus reflected in the composition of the painting too, a strategy which clearly emphasizes the effect of the picture, its inner tension and aesthetic. From time to time it has been pointed out that Leonardo and Bosch are similar in many ways. Both were incredibly inventive and creative, both produced paintings the likes of which had never been seen before, and yet they were complete opposites in terms of their understanding of the world. In this depiction of the hay wain, however, they are united by the "sfumato" of the far-reaching landscape which for the first time in Western painting comes close to the real and actual world.

In the right wing (29), hell, Bosch returns to the theme of the triptych. In this hell which is not a place but a spiritual condition, a strange and at the same time absurd contradiction strikes the eye. While the town in the background blazes away, black clouds of smoke rise, and everything is breaking apart and being destroyed, people continue building the large tower in the centre, an action which is as senseless as it is foolish (56). The boundless stupidity of mankind, highlighted in the paradise of the left wing and continued in the central compartment, is again confirmed in hell. Infernal and gruesome demon figures lead the faceless humans towards their deserved punishment. These people are as distant in hell, however, as they are elsewhere. Although they are exposed to terrible tortures, are skewered and eaten, they do not seem to suffer but continue their labours undisturbed. The naked human figure, led away by two cat-like demons at the bottom of the picture, is interesting. Just as those expelled from paradise look back one last time and still do not grasp their misdeed, or look longingly at the lost paradise, so this figure casts one last glance at the hay wain procession. Robbed of all human pomp, of the proud garments and the avariciously gathered goods, it looks back one last time before being led to its execution. But this creature cannot suffer either, it is not actually present. If paradise is a place of bliss and the hay wain a place of illusions, then hell can only logically be understood as a place of truth.

Bosch expresses intellectual matters in the painting by applying the means of the real world and his imagination. This fact makes them so frightening, so magical and yet not as final and frightful as the first impressions gained from the painting would lead one to suppose. At the centre of hell stands the mighty tower. As in numerous other paintings by Bosch, the depiction of towers plays an important symbolic role. Either they are purely constructions inspired by his vivid imagination which point to the unrealness of the towns and the world; or they are, as is mainly the case, allusions to the Tower of Babel. Although by that time Gothic cathedral towers were already long since well known, Bosch adheres here to the traditional custom of depicting Babylonian towers in a Romanesque manner, such that the tower becomes a symbol and a sign. It is the work of the devilish demons and an allegory of human madness and the arrogant self-deception of man. The doomed souls enter this tower, with the result that it is constantly increasing in size, as is shown by the devilish figures who continue to build busily. Written sources see in this refuge of pride and vice a living tower made up of the bodily souls of all sinners. These living stones stand in striking contrast to the faithful believers in God's community whose souls make up the church. Architecture, landscape and nature are thus worked into a complex system of symbols, in the "Hay Wain" triptych as in many other paintings by this unique artist, a system fashioned by the unprecedented imagination of the Master.

57   The Ship of Fools
Oil on panel, 57.8 x 32.5 cm. Paris, Louvre
The "Ship of Fools" was once supposed to become part of a triptych too, with both other parts also being devoted to the theme of the "Ship of Fools". Once again Bosch takes on the task of the depiction of human weaknesses, as he does also in the treatment of "Gluttony and Lust" (60) and "The Cure of Folly". So the vices of mankind, alongside the depiction of biblical themes, enter the foreground of his mind, and in this genre too Bosch steps out onto new paths in the depiction of these qualities. As representatives of mankind, a few citizens of this earth have climbed into a nutshell and set sail for their destruction. Neither the position of their craft nor the journey itself represents the focus of their foolish action, but solely their pleasure in gluttony, music and trivial pursuits. The strange barge is hopelessly overloaded, even incapable of manoeuvre, for in the place of the sail we see a bush and a treetop to which a chicken is tied which one fool wishes to cut down. From the leaves the sneering face of a devil grins, to whom the crescent on the flag also alludes. So this company of fools sails under the sign of the devil. (Already in the painting "Christ presented to the People" (34) the town is marked as a homestead of the devil by its Satanic flag with the crescent.)
The group of travellers here is made up of people from the most important classes in society of that time: the drunken monk listens to the guitar-playing of the lustful nun, ordinary citizens and craftsmen stumble around blindly; some have already landed in the sea and attempt to climb into the boat again. Other painters and writers have explored the theme of the Ship of Fools too, such that it has been exceedingly popular. In Bosch's case, this collection of fools is a symbol of the whole of mankind which, thanks to its foolishness and blindness, wanders around the world without any sense of direction. The ship, as a symbol of life on this earth and of human stupidity, passes frighteningly before steep mountains. So the tragi-comical situation of these travellers becomes even clearer because for the inhabitants of the Netherlands, mountains, something mostly unknown to them, were a symbol of fear and of loss of direction, a loss of direction which seems to have befallen this ship's party too.
Finally, it should be pointed out that not only the "Ship of Fools" is depicted here; the perversion of an old Christian symbol is just as significant. The ship has always been regarded as a Christian symbol. In the sea of vice and sin, God's ship passes safely through the floods to arrive in one piece as the new "Noah's Ark" at its goal, paradise. Bosch adopts this symbol, combines it with heathen connotations and so gives it a new atomicity which can be understood on the whole as a moralizing condemnation. For Bosch, the world is a boat populated by fools, on which all kinds of madness and foolishness take place, and man is as stupid as the quack in "The Cure of Folly". The effect of Bosch's paintings should not be seen, however, in the moralizing condemnation and the interpretation of human vices. Certainly, this lamentation stands at the centre of his at times pessimistic interpretation of the boggy path walked by mankind. But Bosch was not alone with this view. Wherever you looked at that time preachers with sharp tongues were on their way, holding a mirror up to mankind in a truly drastic manner. Unlike these preachers, Bosch found new forms and ways to formulate his message and present it clearly to the people in the form of his pictures. Nevertheless, his paintings remain, if one divides them up according to the various levels of meaning, indecipherable, i.e. unreadable, on some of these levels. Precisely this unreadable quality bewings our imagination, stimulates us to work towards new, quite personal interpretations. Bosch gives us a clue, points us in a direction which everyone can follow for himself. His paintings invite us to linger, to meditate, to chuckle. Much is explicable, much remains concealed, and only our secret and in part subconscious fears and desires can respond to these cosmic visions.

59   The Vagabond
Oil on panel, 71 x 70.6 cm. Rotterdam, Museum Boymans-van Beuningen
If Bosch uses his paintings of the lives of the saints as a vehicle for describing man's capacity for deciding between Good and Evil, and his freedom to do so, then he varies this moralizing theme here in favour of a depiction which relates to the Old Testament. The vagabond – the prodigal son – is of course not depicted in terms of the historical reality but within the framework of the present of the artist, Bosch. He draws a picture of life at that time, shows us the customs, costumes and architecture of his home territory. Alongside the formal analysis we see, as in numerous other works by Bosch, elements of folklore which enable us to come to conclusions about the existence of peasants and the bourgeois at that time. For this interpretation the landscape is undoubtedly important also; this element of topography and historiography has its value too. Bosch enlightens us on the subject of the appearance of towns and of architectonics, he gives us some idea of farming, vegetation and fauna.
These levels of the painting can all be decoded simply by looking at them. If we wish to penetrate further levels of meaning in this painting, as in other paintings, however, we require for this purpose some knowledge
of iconology, i.e. the science of how symbols and meanings interrelate. In the picture of the prodigal son, the poorly dressed farmer's son faces the decision of whether he should re-enter his father's land (on the right) or return to the inn and brothel (left); once again we have here a variation on the theme of Good and Evil, dressed up in an incident or story from the Old Testament. The ominous inn, the dirty den of vice, is gradually deteriorating. The roof is damaged, the windows shattered, the shutters off their hinges. At the entrance Ladies of Pleasure are laughing at the fallen suitor and apparently want to persuade him to return. The swan (on the inn's sign), the dog and the pigs are not only decoration, but simultaneously symbols of stupidity, gluttony and vanity. The stumbling vagabond stops and looks back; for a moment he wishes to turn and not go back to his father, to virtue and respectability. If he turns to the right, happiness and security are promised to him. This is indicated by the pig's foot which hangs on his jacket and is supposed to bring good luck. If he decides in favour of vice and evil, he must reckon with ill fortune. This is indicated by the cat's fur in his basket. The spoon marks the prodigal son as a spendthrift and waster. Written sources have informed us how the story ended; but do we know how we would decide in a similar situation?
This level of meaning in the painting can only be decoded if the individuals signs are read correctly and in a certain context. Without such knowledge or with a different understanding of them, we could read a meaning into the work which the artist did not intend. It could be a poor peasant who leaves his farm to earn money away from his home area in order to be able to repair his house and feed his family. Certainly that would be a possible, but given the overall context surely not an accurate, interpretation of the painting.

60   The Allegory of Gluttony and Lust
Oil on panel, 31 x 35 cm. Yale University, USA, Art Gallery
Once again in his work Bosch explores the vices and foolishness of man. In this relatively small painting he shows two cardinal sins of mankind in general: gluttony and lust. It is supposed that these pictures once belonged to a series which portrayed the seven Deadly Sins and which was created for a well-known family of the Netherlandish nobility. The coat of arms on the roof of the tent provides evidence for this theory. In addition, we recognize on the roof the sign which juts out with a stylized pig's foot. It alludes to lust to which the loving couple in the tent surrender. The couple have taken the precaution of depositing their sword, hat and slippers outside the tent, which again are symbols of lust. The difficulty of interpreting symbols of this kind is illustrated by a painting by van Eyck in which the slippers (shoes) before the couple means that the male is under the thumb of the female, which, of course, could also be the case here; perhaps she has initiated this secret meeting in the summerhouse. At the top of the picture, a carnival-like figure, a drunken, potbellied citizen, is riding on a floating barrel from which the wine is pouring into the dish of another drunkard. In this lake bathed in wine we recognize three further fellows who push the barrel through the floods, and a swimming clergyman whose (bishop's) hat has fallen down over his forehead. It would appear that after enjoying the wine he is drifting around, blind and helpless.
Possibly Bosch wished here to ridicule not just the social class of the average citizen but also those with the rank of the clergy.

63   St John on Patmos
Oil on panel, 63 x 43.3 cm. Berlin-Dahlem, Gemäldegalerie
This work depicts "St John on Patmos"; on the reverse we see scenes from Christ's Passion (not illustrated here). This picture belongs to a series of depictions of

saints which includes "St Jerome at Prayer" (62), "St John the Baptist in the Wilderness" (58), and "St Christopher" (61). Consequently, we can discern a third thematic group in the oeuvre of Hieronymus Bosch.
Together with depictions of the Life and Passion of Christ, pictorial interpretations of the lives of the saints represent a significant area of medieval art. It is not so much the model of Christ, of the Holy Trinity, which stands at the centre of the Church syllabus, but the lives of the saints. These men and women play an important role in daily Christian life for they place their complete lives in God's keeping and act in accordance with the rules formulated in the Bible. Many paid for their faith in Jesus in the form of humiliation, torture and death, and so became models to be imitated. They knew how to resist vice and sin, despite all the temptations of the devil, and so Bosch busies himself intensively with the description of these very virtues, for the Master was already practised in this art: in the illustration and interpretation of human vices and diabolical temptations. But if the saints resist the attempts of the devil to worm himself into their favour, the citizens on earth succumb to these temptations in grotesque fashion.
St John sits in his elegant and flowing robe on a rock and listens to the divine inspiration of the Mother of God, who appears before him, floating on a cloud. He has been meditating and has this contemplation to thank for his divine enlightenment and inspiration. Mary is not present in real terms, but is a reference to the dialogue between Mary and God. The book, i.e. the Bible, by the rules of which he lives, allows him in the first place to hear these words. If the book in this painting is a reference to enlightenment and truth, then the book on the head of the monk in the picture "The Cure of Folly" appears to be the opposite, the book of stupidity: it is closed. While the saint listens to the melodies of the Mother of Jesus, a demon, disguised as a beetle, comes secretly and stealthily closer to steal the saint's inkwell with a rake. Were this to succeed, John would no longer be in a position to commit the divine inspiration to paper. To the left of the holy man we recognize, however, the emblem of St John, i.e. the eagle who checks the thief. This story, above all these symbols of this drawing, can be traced back to descriptions of the Apocalypse and to medieval manuscripts which Bosch reproduces here in unadulterated form. Whereas in his other large cycles of paintings Bosch ventures out onto completely new paths, he remains largely faithful to tradition in his depictions of saints. Bosch researchers point not only to literary sources but also to related models, e.g. Martin Schongauer, Dierk Bouts and Diests. The landscape painting in these works proves just as traditional. It is a Netherlandish coastal region, pleasing to the eye, with a rich merchant city in the background. No catastrophes of any description, no great fires, no floods characterize the "Italian landscape"; rather we see an intact world formed according to the Christian rules of creation. Whereas Bosch, in his interpretations of vice and of the "Last Day", selects his landscape either to emphasize decline on this earth, or as a contrast to that, as is the case here, unbroken harmony typifies this painting. The landscape has thus become decoration, more of a stage setting, which accompanies, indeed interprets, the staged action.
On the reverse of the painting we recognize a circle painted on a dark background in which scenes from the Passion of Christ are depicted (not illustrated here). This roundel represents the earth, floating in the dark nothingness of the universe, of a universe which is not blue, as is usual, but in which the light, i.e. Jesus, has faded. The colours in which the flow of scenes from Christ's bitter path to the cross are executed thus seem dark too. Bosch, in this appendix, introduces us to a really wretched landscape in which the Lord's end takes place. Bare rocks, dried-up meadows and fields, and an apparently dead ghost-town – Jerusalem – form the sad scenery for this drama. The cycle begins with the crucifixion on the mountain of Golgotha and ends with the burial of Christ. Mary and John are left behind on the barren hill, while the crowd has already withdrawn, for on the far horizon a terrible storm and floods have announced their impending arrival. In both the scenes at the bottom we see Christ before Pilate and the Mocking of Christ. Hope appears in the centre of the roundel: a pelican gives its young to drink of its own blood. This is a very old reference to the Passion, to the sacrifice of blood, and so too to salvation. The young sit on a large rock and are a symbol for the young congregation of the Church. This community of which Christ said, "You are Peter and on this rock I will build my church", represents not only the very beginning of the church but also a refuge of divine salvation.

62 St Jerome in Prayer

Oil on panel, 77 x 59 cm. Ghent, Musée des Beaux Arts
The saint has discarded all the worldly insignia of wealth and power as a sign of penance and cast himself to the ground in a hair shirt. Beside him we see a hat, a closed book – possibly a symbol of foolishness –, a cloak and a broken globe which points to the destruction of everything of this earth. Jerome has drawn back completely from worldly goods and closes his eyes. Like St John, he practises meditation and dialogue with God. He wants nothing to do with the world which at first sight is pleasing to the eye, for despite its beautiful and seductive external appearance it is not suited for leading man to God. Not only the already mentioned symbols point to this interpretation by Bosch, but also the tablets of stone which emerge from the rock. They are the broken laws of Moses and, like the lizard, the dog, and the owl, symbols of the devil on earth.
The landscape serves the interpretation of the action in this work too, is the scenery and the stage simultaneously. Gradually this otherwise friendly "paysage" turns into demonic images, into visions, which we might see nowadays too, given a certain mood or light conditions. The penitent who chastises himself is so deep in prayer that Christ appears to him; in the picture we see the "living" Redeemer, who is not a piece of wood or iron, but is in the process of becoming flesh again. Bosch combines in his depiction of the saint and the landscape several ideas which overlap: the narrative points to an event in the life of St Jerome, the allegorical elements are designed to make the spectator aware of the deeper meaning of the painting by means of symbols, e.g. the broken stone tablets. The instructive component encompasses these meanings and combines them to form a moral statement which can be traced back to the text of the gospel.

58 St John the Baptist in the Wilderness

Oil on panel, 48.5 x 40 cm. Madrid, Museo Lazaro Gagliano
As in the depiction of his other saints, Bosch selects here clearly contrasting colours: the brown-green landscape which stretches from the foreground deep into the background; and the purple-red of the cloak. This complementary contrast leads us straight to the meaning of the painting, for the difference between the landscape and the saint corresponds to the opposing colours. John has spread himself out comfortably on a luscious meadow, his upper body rests on a rock covered with moss. His heavy bearded head is supported by one raised hand. John has almost closed his tired eyes and he is dreaming. What he is dreaming, we cannot see, for on the mere surface no indication is given. We must descend into deeper, allegorical levels of meaning in order, gradually, to see behind the deceptively attractive landscape. John is sunk deep in meditation and turns his thoughts to God, to whom the lamb in the bottom right hand corner points. In the picture this indication is expressed indirectly in the shape of the Lamb of God, Jesus, and of the hand of the holy man who points to it. To this extent, Bosch follows the traditional interpretation of the scene which, however, he now expands in his own sense. John is dreaming or meditating not only about God and his teaching; his thoughts sometimes drift to the desires of the flesh and to the temptations offered by the world. He is standing, so to speak, at the crossroads between virtue and vice, he must decide between good and evil. The devil does the dirty on him, and Bosch shows us here how difficult it was not only for the saint to decide. We too must decide, for John the Baptist paid for his faith in God with his death, as we know from the New Testament. Once again Bosch conceals a moral condemnation behind the obvious depiction. The fantastically fashioned plant in the foreground points to the temptations of vice. It is a sign of sexual desires and dreams. Birds pick the seed from the large, well-rounded and full fruits which offer themselves to the spectator. Eve too reached for the forbidden fruit, for vice and sin, and was expelled from paradise. However, this plant is not only a symbol of the sexually seductive arts of the female, but also a sign for nature as a whole which distracts man from meditation and contemplation. Bosch takes nature and its earthly goods and makes them responsible for all that is bad in man. For this reason too the saint cannot decide at the moment of temptation whether to open or close his eyes.

61 St Christopher

Oil on panel, 113 x 71.5 cm. Rotterdam, Museum Boymans-van Beuningen
With a heavy load, St Christopher wades through a river which apparently quite illogically is built into the foreground of a landscape which descends towards the background. Of course, it could also be a lake, for a further slowly flowing stretch of water leads one's gaze into a broad Netherlandish coastal landscape. Already in the painting of John in the wilderness (58), it can be established that the attractive landscape is not a wilderness and has allegorical value. These hills, executed in green, as well as the waters, are scenery and do not have the purpose of pleasing the eye or of an exact representation of a landscape; instead they serve the artist by illustrating the opposition between Good and Evil, between Nature, Man and God. In a manner similar to that employed in the picture of John, Bosch emphasizes the contrast between the saint and the world by means of a striking complementary contrast of the colours red and green.
Christopher has cast back his purple cloak and wades through the floods, supported by his stick. Upon closer inspection we become aware of an illusion: the Infant Jesus is hovering above the saint, so he does not in fact have a weight to bear. It is more a case of the weight of the world, of the burden – in Bosch's view – of having to live virtuously and of rejecting the temptations of this world. The holy man must suffer greatly in the face of this decision, for in the background we see monks and hermits who surrender themselves to the joys of life. Naked figures savour the bliss of bathing and sexual desires before a ruin, and in the foreground, to the right, clergymen who have succumbed to gluttony descend upon a tree. In this tree, made leafless in a queer way, we recognize a wine jug and a large beehive. The monks have lost themselves among the bare branches and harvest honey and flesh, which again are symbols of gluttony and sexual desire. A proud cock keeps guard beneath a dry tree, a cock which symbolizes the betrayal of Christ, just as the clergy have betrayed their teaching by surrendering themselves to earthly delights.

30 The Martyrdom of St Ontcommer

Oil on panel, 104 x 63 cm; wings 104 x 28 cm. Venice, Palazzo Ducale
The "Martyrdom of St Ontcommer" is a middle-sized triptych; the main part describes the crucifixion of the saint in rich colours and expressive forms. On the side wings, which are in poor condition, are new variations on the theme "bad world": slave-dealers, ships cracking apart in a storm, and a blazing town. We see here a depiction of virtue and vice, such as can be found in the great triptychs by Bosch.

The composition of the painting is strictly geometrical. The high and heavy cross, which reaches almost to the top of the picture, divides the painting into two equal parts. To the left and to the right, the citizens attending the crucifixion are arranged in the form of acute-angled triangles. It is a classical composition of Italian origin, something extremely rare in the work of Bosch. The inner rhythm of the painting bears the stamp of Italian and of Netherlandish traditions (van Eyck). Compositions, character rhythm and colouring lend the painting a monumental nature, unusual for Bosch, which becomes visible too in the division of the hilly landscape in the background. Both groups of figures in the foreground and centre are set off by the arrangement of rocks on both sides in the background. Spiritualized and hardly suffering, the saint looks down from the cross. It would appear that she is not crucified but has opened her arms wide to greet God, to absorb what he stands for. She is magnificently dressed in order to appear proud and composed before Jesus. Dazzled by her radiance and inner strength, the tormentors stagger into one another and can hardly grasp the miracle. To the right, the treacherous governors, the City Fathers, are ashamed of the senselessness of their violence. Bewildered, the chaotic crowds flee, some hide their faces, others faint. As can be seen, Bosch here condemns all social classes for their disgraceful actions: magnificently dressed citizens and clergymen are equally responsible for the bloody deed.

64   The Seven Deadly Sins
Oil on panel, 120 x 150 cm. Madrid, Prado

This work was originally painted on a tabletop; only at a later date was it decided that the picture should be viewed vertically. In terms of composition it resembles a circular painting, i.e. a "tondo". Inherent in the tondo is the significance of the circle, of the wheel, which, in symbolic terms, stands for the world itself. Within the context of this world, Bosch tells the story of the Seven Deadly Sins; medieval notions on virtue had meant that until then the deadly sins had always been presented in didactic fashion opposite the cardinal virtues. Bosch excludes the virtues from his painting and thus elucidates one of his central messages: for him, the world, i.e. the world of man, is, on the whole, bad. The institutions of the Church, like the secular institutions, and the bourgeoisie just like all other levels of society, have fallen to Satan's temptations. The round picture recalls also the wheel of fortune and the lottery wheel, both related to the circle, both interpreted as a symbol of life. Wherever the wheel stops, the spectator sees only illustrations of sins; there are no sections which point to virtue, or promise happiness.

At the centre of the painting, Christ, resurrected, appears, surrounded by rays of brilliant sunlight. The sun and Jesus are at the centre not just of this painting, but of the world in general. From this central position God can see everything which is happening on earth; consequently, he raises his hand in warning and advises caution – he passes on to the spectator the penetrating message that God sees everything. In Bosch's description, man commits the seven deadly sins more or less randomly, and hardly listens to the word of God. He blindly succumbs to the frivolous vices and sins which are the theme of almost all Bosch's work. Self-deception, errors, blindness, and arrogance are characteristics which the artist presents to the spectator, as though he were holding up a mirror, such that we might open our eyes. If one views this painting from a distance, it looks at first like a convex mirror, in the manner familiar to us from other pictorial works of art from the 16th and 17th century. The mirror shows daily and banal events as though we ourselves were protagonists in the painting; an optical illusion, an error, a delusion, presented by Bosch here as though we are supposed to see ourselves on the glass tabletop. The pictures pass before our eyes, just like on a turning "panopticum": envy, covetousness, gluttony, anger, pride, lust, and sloth. We recognize lusting lovers; a clergyman who has fallen asleep before a fire; a fat bourgeois; a corrupt judge; angry, fighting peasants; a miser hungry for more money; envious businessmen interested in other men's goods; and a proud and vain wife of a bourgeois. These vices (sins) are distributed among the secular and the religious in a manner which reflects the frequency with which each group indulges in the various vices. The classification remains interchangeable, however, for these are actually random extracts from daily life, then and now. Not just the world, but above all its notions of morals and morality, have undergone a serious loss of equilibrium; we observe a "loss of the middle ground" in general.

Four further round pictures accompany the circle; in these, Bosch presents to us the "Four Last Things". From Death, man marches towards the Resurrection (top right), before then being placed before the Court on the "Last Day" (bottom right). An extremely hard and inevitable judgement is passed: man ends up in Hell. In unmistakable terms, Bosch here suggests that our path through life has a pessimistic tenor. The great triptychs develop this theme and present splendid artistic allegories, in which the Court Session is only mentioned in passing, as it were, and more space is devoted to the depiction of Hell. Just as, in many cases, there is no court in this world, and there is hardly such a thing as a fair judgement, so too in these pictures, mankind is not given a chance in the life to come. As Bosch sees it, Hell or eternal purgatory is the state to which our souls will fall or have already fallen, as though in a day-dream.

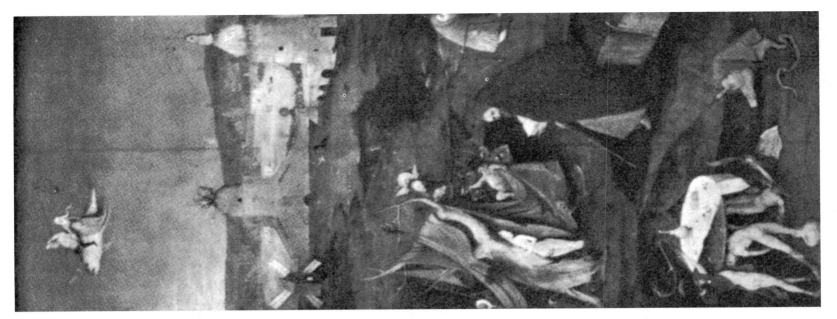

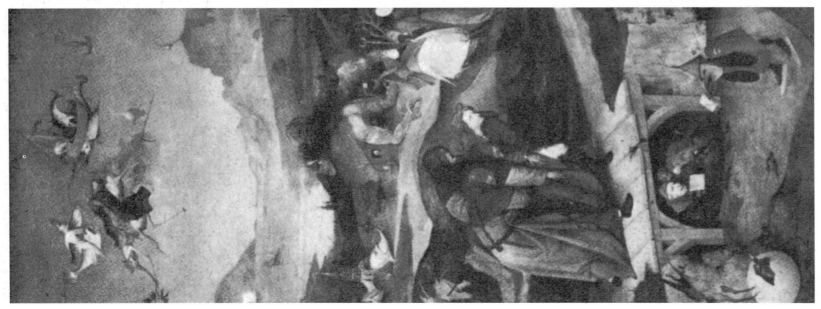

The Colour Plates

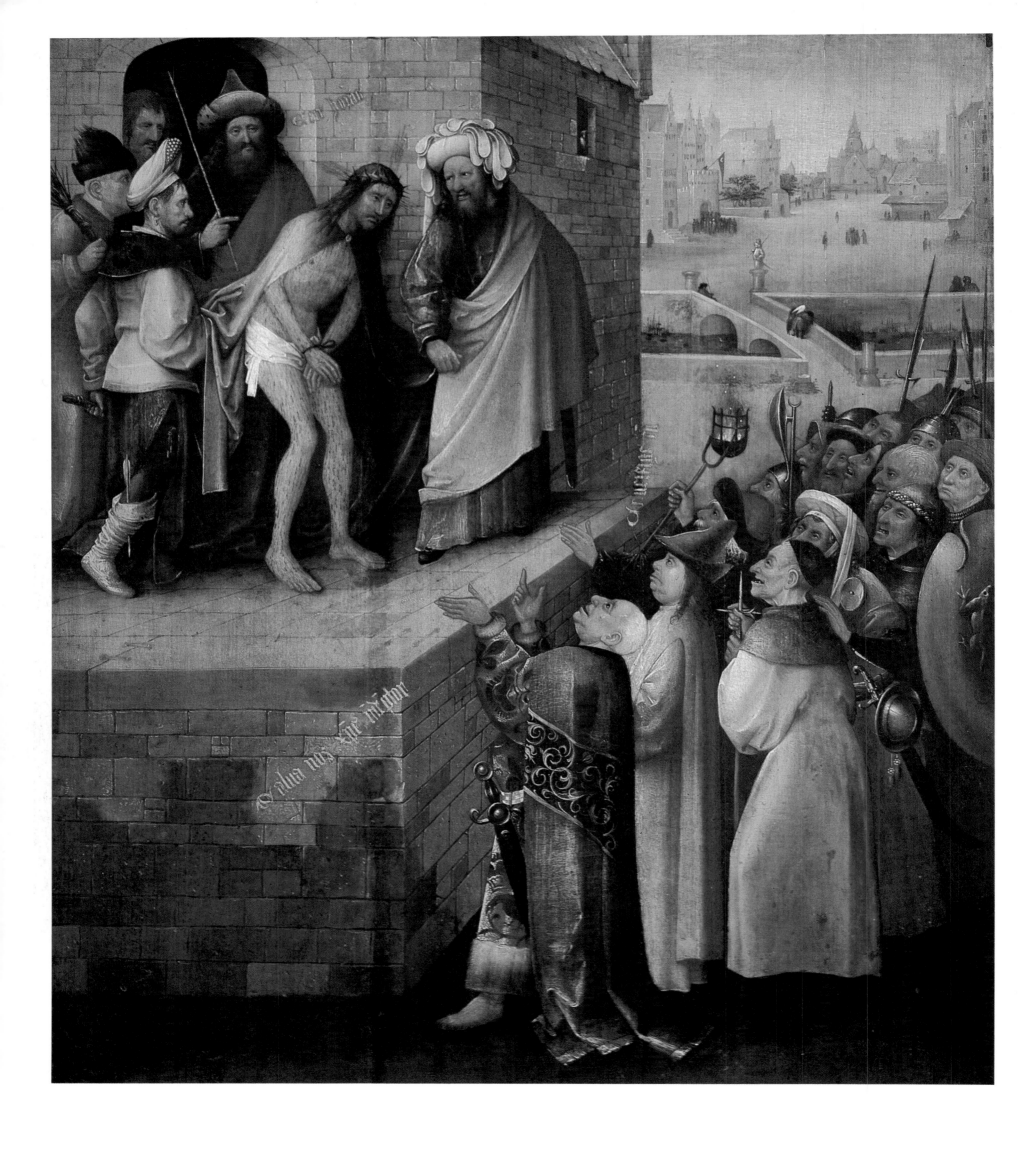

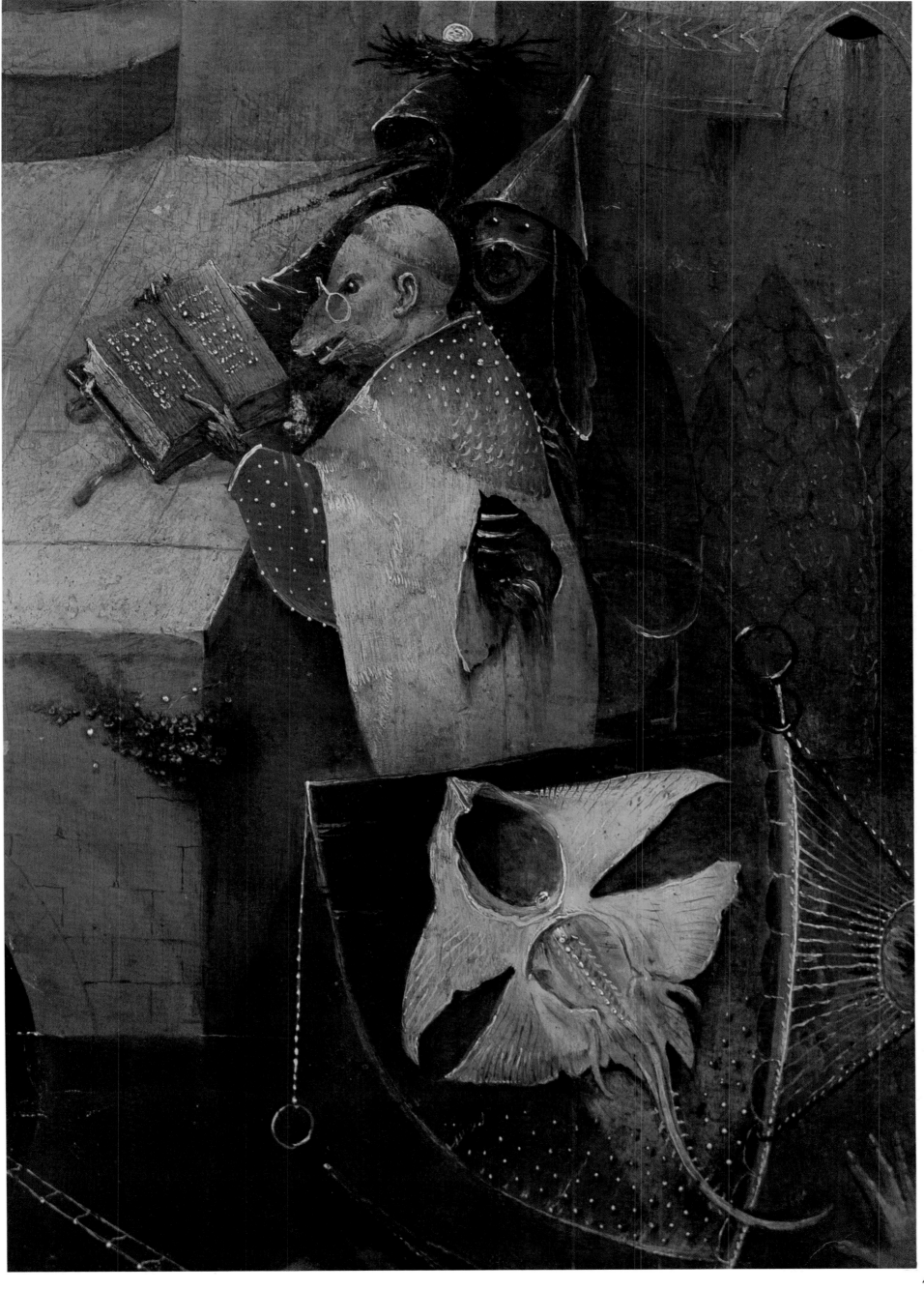

48

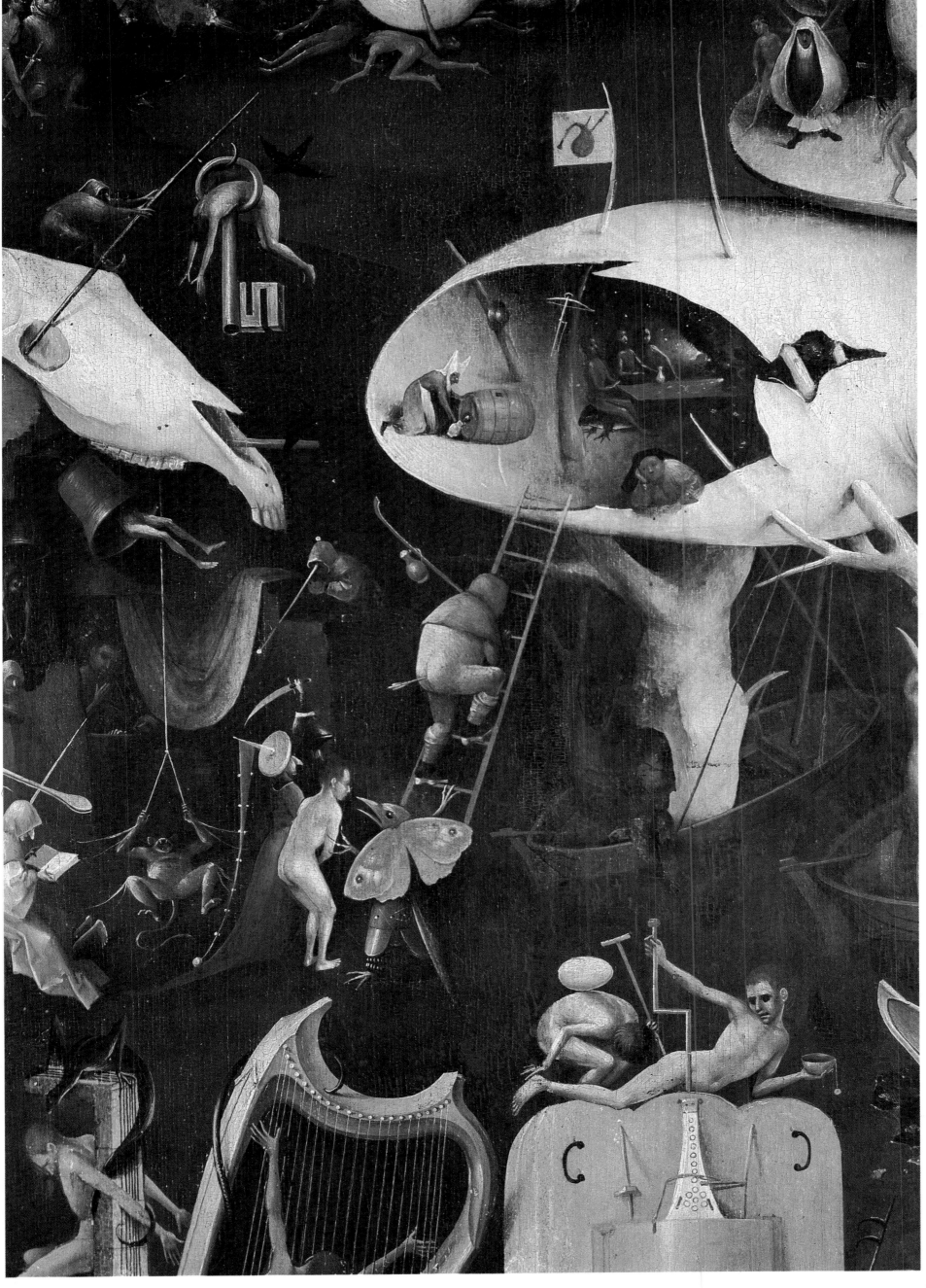

1079 JHERONIMUS BOSCH · DE VERLOREN ZOON · ca 1450 - 1516